#GHETTO
THE INNER CITY
BLUES

Thaddeus Tolbert

First Printing: 2019

ISBN: 978-0-359-12369-8

DEDICATION

This book is dedicated to all my people in every ghetto across the map. Shout out to South Park, Yellowstone, 4th ward, 5th ward, 3rd ward, and the whole city of Houston. For all the ones who are on lock, still on the block, in high school earning their diploma, in college earning their degree, or no longer here to tell their stories. The first-generation changers and difference makers who do not get the credit they deserve, this is for you, too. To all the people who have ever been written off by the day ones who said they will forever ride by your side. For everyone who has ever been short changed or taken advantage of, this is for you. R.I.P. my loved ones and your loved ones that are keeping guard of the ghetto from heaven. I appreciate everyone who is taking the time to read and comprehend my side of the story. By the end of this book, if you do not already, you will RESPECT THE GHETTO! This is my story of the blues of my people, for the people.

CONTENTS

1. When It Was All Good   Pg. 1

2. Is It Still All Good?   Pg. 16

3. The Family Divides   Pg. 25

4. Soul Food   Pg. 39

5. Cold Nights with No Lights   Pg. 60

6. The Lion's Den   Pg. 73

7. Class of '10   Pg. 87

8. The Struggle Continues   Pg. 107

9. Risking My Life   Pg. 128

10. Back Trippin'   Pg. 143

11. About My Brothers Business   Pg. 164

12. Reincarnated   Pg. 177

13. Perseverance/Be Humble   Pg. 187

14. My Side of the Story   Pg. 202

CHAPTER 1
WHEN IT WAS ALL GOOD

"Wake up, time to get ready for school!"

I recognized the soft voice and touch of my mama as the sun peeked through my curtains. I tried to find every reason not to get up for school as I lied comfortably in the bed stretching. Before I even realized it, I drifted off to sleep with a Kool-Aid smile on my face. That mini slumber ended when I heard my granny's house shoes sliding across the floor. I jumped out of the bed and hit the floor as if gunshots were ringing out nearby. I probably had a flashback of the gunshots I heard the night before.

"Boy, you heard your mama . . . get your ass up and get ready for school!"

On this day, I believe I broke the record time for making up a bed, taking a bath, brushing my teeth and getting dressed. My granny was no taller than 5'3" but had a right hook and jab like Mike Tyson and George Foreman all in one. The good Lord knows I was not trying to get my ass whooped before school.

I walked into my parent's room every morning like clockwork to stand in front of the mirror and imitate my daddy. He would rub his hands as he checked out his outfit; he just knew he was fresh every time he walked away from the mirror. I can still smell that bold scent of Fahrenheit by Christian Dior that lingered long after he left the house.

As I stood before the mirror, I thought to myself, "Got damn! I should be able to pull Kedrah's number today if I smell good like this." I knew damn well my daddy told me not to touch anything of his without his permission, but I was not worried about the consequences; I had Kedrah's fine ass on my mind. To me, Kedrah was the most beautiful girl I had ever seen and I was crushing hard as hell. I drenched myself in the cologne and went to eat my breakfast. Mama Bea was in the kitchen throwing down on biscuits, sausage, grits and scrambled eggs.

My mama's soft voice transformed into an annoying scream as she yelled, "Thadd, come on; we're going to be late! You can take that in the car with you."

Damn, so much for enjoying my breakfast in peace.

Thinking about the way my mama hit corners when she was in a hurry, I figured all the food would be on my school clothes and on the floor. *How can I talk to Kedrah or anybody smelling like cologne and cane syrup?* I had to pass on my granny's biscuits that day and settle for the breakfast served at school.

"Have a good day at school today, son, and your teacher better not call me about a damn thing today either."

Mama knew I would be in class cutting up with the guys and my conduct card would be either on red or white; red meant you acted a fool that day, but white meant a phone call home and a possible ass whooping later.

After saying goodbye to my mama, I ran out of the car to catch up with the guys—Josh, Brandon and Lance. We walked into the cafeteria to grab our lunch cards when Brandon leaned in and whispered, "Thadd, bro, there goes Kedrah and her patnas!"

Bro already knew what I was on that day because everyone clearly smelled the strong cologne.

We walked through the line to get breakfast then sat at the table with the girls. Just as I was taking my seat,

Jesse, the ugly girl in class, grabbed me saying, "Oooohhh, Thaddeus you smell good as hell today, baby!"

I pulled away from her in disgust and the guys busted out laughing hard as hell. Jesse had been crushing on me since we were in kindergarten and I had been avoiding her ass ever since. I eventually took my seat next to Kedrah embarrassed beyond measure. The guys were still laughing and cracking jokes; they even reminisced about the time Jesse kissed me on the bus during a field trip.

That flashback ended when Kedrah touched my hand. "Yes, Thaddeus, you do smell good."

I must have had the craziest smile on my face again because she was smiling and laughing hard. Guess that Fahrenheit did what it was supposed to do because she not only touched me and smiled but also gave me her number.

The bell rang for us to go to class, so we dumped our trays and continued with our day.

That day was a good day because the finest girl in class gave me her number and I did not have to change the color of my conduct card, not even once. The teacher was amazed that I remained attentive and on task that day.

Before I knew it, the three o'clock dismissal bell rang and we ran to the front of the school to meet our rides home. That is when I finally considered the consequences of putting on my daddy's cologne. I noticed my father in the car waiting on my little sister and me like clockwork at 3:05 p.m. Boy, my heart raced like I was back in P.E. class. That ass whooping was on my mind, but I thought, *Fuck it; I'll call Kedrah once I'm settled in.*

"What's up son . . . hey baby girl." Daddy greeted us as we entered the car. He was blasting and bobbing his head to his Geto Boys CD as we drove to the store to get dinner for the night. I sat in relief because he did not say anything about the cologne. Hell, I even started to bob my head hard and rapped along with Scarface during his verse.

We bought our groceries and went home so that my daddy and granny could start dinner while my sister and I completed our homework. After I entered my room and unpacked my bag to do my homework, my daddy walked in taking his belt off.

"Your ass thought I didn't know you was in my cologne, huh?"

Before I could say anything, that six feet even two-hundred-pound man armed with a thick ass leather belt flew across the room and beat the scent off my ass. My daddy had twenty-inch biceps, so that whip action was something serious. I could not sit down like a normal person for a good three days. I did not even want to call Kedrah anymore as I still felt the sting from that beatdown.

I wanted to say to hell with that homework as well, but my daddy asserted, "You better start on that homework before I start whooping on that ass again!"

My daddy's voice is deep like Mufasa from *The Lion King* and his face is as stern as a Native American; which is evidently in our bloodline because my grandfather and grandmother had the same look. The crazy part is, I already thought of my daddy and me as Mufasa and Simba. It would make perfect sense if you saw the crazy things I did and how he got on my ass with no hesitation.

Eventually my mama came home and from the look on my face, she knew I had gotten my ass whooped. She twisted her face at me, shook her head, and greeted my daddy with a hug and kiss as he sipped on a cold can of Miller Lite. She entered the kitchen to fix our plates as my daddy lectured me on why he whooped my ass and once again told me the importance of asking permission to use anything that does not belong to me. He said what I did was considered stealing, which was against the law, and God was going to punish me worse than he could. That is when I thought about the story Brandon told me about how his brother got caught stealing and went to jail. I had heard several stories about jail being that practically all my cousins had been to juvenile detention, jail or prison. I knew I did not want to take that route, but I thought I had to be like my daddy to get girls. He thought I was green to the game, but I noticed how the ladies used to look at him in the grocery store.

I admitted to my father why I used the cologne and he dropped his head to laugh.

"You're my son and just like me. I already knew why you did what you did before you even said anything about it." He then began to tell me pick-up lines and player things to say when talking to a woman. As he was getting into his player ass days from Yates and after, my mama walked back into the room and my daddy changed the subject quicker than a dope fiend could scale a fence. My mama did not say anything but from the look on her face, I knew she had overheard my daddy's story.

My ass was still sore, but I enjoyed the dinner and quality time I had with my family. Just when it was getting good, 8:30 p.m. came knocking at the door; which meant it was time to bathe and prepare for bed before nine o'clock. My mama got my little sister and baby brother ready for bed as I hurried to my granny's room to pray and kiss her good night.

I lied in bed but could not sleep. It was as quiet as a mouse as I stared at my ceiling. Although only eight years old, I thought about life and what I wanted to be when I grew up. Daddy made sure he kept us up on game at an early age, so I was way ahead of my time cognitively. Just like everyone else in my ghetto, I had to grow up fast being the eldest child of my parents. I had to lead by example, which I did, but most of my peers did not, so they often emulated the images of our ghetto.

I also thought about how most of the guys from school talked about how they either did not know who their fathers were or how their fathers were either in jail or dead. I cried as I thought about how fortunate I was and wished I could share my daddy with everyone in the hood. In 3rd Ward, many of us had drug dealers, pimps, jack boys and athletes to idolize; I had my daddy. He emphasized how I had no choice but to go to college because he did not go and he wanted me to be a better man than him. Some of my friends had never even heard of college and we had two right in the heart of the ghetto. Survival was the story for everyone whether you had both parents in your household or not. That left a bad taste in my mouth because I did not want any of my people to suffer or fall victim to the hood.

The yells of the people that walked the streets at night and the sounds of dogs barking interrupted my thoughts. Those yells and barks quickly turned into gunshots. The sounds of pistols and AK-47s filled the air and pierced the silence. Police sirens and screeching tires overpowered the sounds of the gunshots. My thoughts then switched to the chaos right under my own roof.

From the outside looking in, my household looked like the ideal family home. You had to live at 2509 to really understand the deal, though. My daddy is a man of solid principles and ran his house accordingly. Anyone that approached those front steps had to come correct or risk using those same steps to leave. My mama is a good woman and came home every night unlike some of my peers' mamas. Whatever she did before she got home and while she was there would somehow trigger my daddy's temper. I saw my daddy slap my mama once and it surprised the hell out of me. After that night, he made sure I knew how wrong it was, adding it to my list of lessons for being a better man than him.

I know my daddy loved my mama but no matter what he said, I could not understand how he could raise his hand to hit her. His anger made us walk around on eggshells because we did not want to be the next target. It seemed as if one minute we were a big happy family, then the next we were running from the gunshots sounding off in our house. My granny often came to the rescue and got on my daddy's ass with no regard. She let it be known that he may be the man of the house, but it was still her house and she was not having all that drama.

I thank God for my granny because she kept Daddy off our asses plenty of times. Her short ass backed down from no one and did not care how big you were; she would come through and check something with the quickness. She was on our asses, too, but she did not get carried away like my daddy would.

It was midnight, I still could not sleep and I had to be up at 7:00 a.m. to get ready for school. I noticed the police lights flashing on my wall, so I assumed another brother from the hood either got killed or arrested. I already knew I would hear the story at school if the shooting did not make the news. Nine times out of ten, it would not be featured on the news; you would just see the blood stains on the street and the yellow police tape. Someone's son, daddy, uncle, brother or friend would not make it back home that night.

As I lied there, I wondered why life had to be so sad, unfair and hectic. As young as I was, I had a lot of questions about this life we live, and about a man named

God. Sometimes this curiosity got me into some trouble that I could not escape, but I just wanted to understand. I told myself I was not going to worry about it and that I needed to enjoy this time to myself. Right before I fell asleep that night, I asked myself, *Is it still all good?*

CHAPTER 2
IS IT STILL ALL GOOD?

The next day arrived and it was time to get dressed for school again. I caught the news with my Uncle Greg as I laced up my shoes.

"Gunshots went off at the intersection of Live Oak and McGowen in the 3rd Ward last night that left one man dead and four others injured. Houston Police are still on the scene investigating but believe the motive of the shooting was drug related."

I sat there thinking, *Damn . . . that's right up the street from my house. I hope that wasn't any of my homeboys or their relatives.*

As we drove up the block on the way to school, we saw the yellow police tape and police cars that blocked off the intersection. This was not the first time I had seen a homicide scene in my ghetto and, sadly, it would not be the last.

At school the guys and I were sitting at the table finishing up breakfast when Brandon asked me, "Say, bro, I heard about that shooting by your house last night. Your people good?"

I replied, "Yeah, man, my people good . . . I've been praying for whoever people that was on the block."

Someone else jumped into the conversation. "Man, I heard that was Lance and them people out there last night."

That explained why Lance was not at the table with us. We all shook our heads in disbelief. We were only in elementary school, but we knew about death, shootouts and drugs all too well.

I lived in the part of the hood known as Dodge City (DC). If you are familiar with the old westerns and cowboy movies, then you will understand the logic. It was common to see a body, blood stains, needles, used condoms or whatever else in the streets. Each section of 3rd Ward is known for something. No matter what or who you are, if you are not from these parts or do not have a pass, then you better keep driving and please do not walk around like something is sweet; someone will pull your card quickly.

My parents were persistent with not allowing my siblings and me to hang around in the streets and serious about us being home when we were supposed to be. Their hard work was not in vain because we never got into any trouble in the streets. No matter how hard they worked, however, we could not avoid developing that ghetto mentality. Going to school with people that were out there in the streets forced you to be hip. You could not be green at all or you would get eaten up for lunch every day. I'd be damned if I looked weak or sweet.

My people also liked us to look nice and presentable and they wanted us to standout. Standing out to them did not involve looking like everyone else, so they did not buy us a lot of Jordan, Air Force Ones, Polo or other designer brands. Even though we owned some designer labels, not many people recognized them. I had friends and associates in school, but that did not stop the other kids from criticizing me simply because my Nikes looked different. They even thought my pants were tight because I did not sag them. At the time, I was not a fighter; I cried a lot and was known as a crybaby. You could not claim the Tre and be a cry baby, so I broke out of that shell slowly and eventually showed them what my hands do.

My daddy taught me a few things about boxing, but I would always jump out there with my older brother and cousins. That is how I learned not to do too much talking: either we were going to fight or go our separate ways. However, I was not trying to get my ass beat at home for starting shit at school. Eventually, we all agreed that the restroom break right after lunch would be the best time to fight. I took some W's and L's but no matter what, we would always end with a handshake and vow not to snitch if someone took an L. I earned my respect this way and I did not have to fight much overtime.

My mama's hands could never measure up to my daddy's, though. We knew to stay out of the way from the fear he instilled in us. My parents always told us to fear only God, but I wondered if God could save us from those beatdowns. *If only they really knew what I went through at 2509, maybe then they wouldn't crack jokes on me anymore.* Every day we faced drama either in the hood or in my house. It was stressful and traumatic as hell but in my house, we were taught if you are a kid, you do not have the right to know or do not know shit about being stressed. Yes, mental health was and still is shortchanged in my ghetto.

All the chaos between my parents continued until my younger sister Taylor's 4th birthday. My mama did something my daddy did not like and he tried to go after her as usual. We sat on the front porch with my granny because she was the go-to person for comfort. The next thing I knew, my mama hurdled over my head. I sat there in disbelief and amazement as I watched my mama sprint down the street. She ran in the direction of the police substation at the end of our street; in that moment I realized she had reached her breaking point.

I held my sister as she cried because she felt like her birthday had been ruined. I knew the feeling all too well because for a while I felt as if our family was crumbling to pieces right before my eyes. About forty-five minutes later, my mama returned to the house in the backseat of a police car and my first thought was, *My daddy is about to go to jail.* I never thought I would see the day my daddy would get arrested and go to prison. Thoughts of all the stories I had heard at school entered my mind along with the feeling I was about to be welcomed into the "my daddy is in jail" club, but that was not even the case. The police questioned my daddy and granny on the events that transpired that day. Because no physical altercation occurred, the police gave my daddy a pass. My mama, however, packed up her things and left.

Not many stories existed about the mama leaving the household; the daddy mostly left in my ghetto. My sister was right about her birthday being ruined, though—the whole day was fucked up. Mama did not say a damn thing to us. She just got into her car and left. I do not know what hurt the most that day, but I know something about my heart was changing. Despite everything, my siblings and I still had each other. I was eight years old, Taylor was four, and my younger brother Lawrence was two.

My daddy held us all that night as we cried. We missed the hell out our mama already and she was not even gone a full twenty-four hours. Daddy explained to us that though he and my mama had their differences, that did not mean they loved us any less. The tears in my sister's eyes and the confusion on my brother's face made me understand much more than any eight-year-old should.

I lied in my bed that night feeling lost, hurt and confused. *What happened to the family that used to go to Hermann Park for picnics, to the beach, and had movie dates at home. I bet root beer floats and homemade burgers taste like the shit I feel like now. I hope Mama is alright and safe out there. I wonder where she is. Does she miss us like we miss her? I just want to hug her and hear her voice right now. I can't stop these tears now because I thought about turning on the news tomorrow morning to see that something had happened to my mama. The trauma of my ghetto and household is fucking with my mind. I guess this is what Bushwick Bill felt like in that Geto Boys song; Aww man homie . . . My mind's playing tricks on me.*

My thoughts along with the fiends on McGowen kept me awake for a while that night. I eventually said a prayer asking God to watch over my mama, family and friends then closed my eyes. *Lord, let this all be a dream and when I wake up in the morning, I will see my mama's smile with the sunshine.*

CHAPTER 3
THE FAMILY DIVIDES

Just when I thought things could not get any worse, worse paid a visit and overstayed her welcome. My daddy got served a subpoena for family court. My mama hired a lawyer, filed for divorce, and requested full custody of us. Damn, I was hoping my mama would be as forgiving as she had always been, but I guess she had had enough of my daddy's shit. Those slaps upside the head and belt welts did hurt like hell, so I could empathize with her. Yes, it was a crazy time, but even crazier is the fact that my daddy recognized his mistakes yet blamed others for the choices he made. He was teaching me about responsibility and accountability not knowing that pointing the finger should have never been a part of the curriculum.

In my mother's absence, the house did not even feel the same anymore. It was filled with people but empty at the same time. I could still hear my mama's voice and it weighed heavily on me. Every time I heard the phone ring, I ran to the phone anticipating her voice only to hear a bill collector or my aunt wanting to talk to Mama Bea about the stories. Whenever I saw a Chevy Lumina, I sped off trying to catch it, but my mama was never in the driver's seat.

I cried to Mama Bea searching for answers, but it seemed as if all she could tell me was to pray and God would make a way. I felt better around Mama Bea because she always had a story to relate to anything you talked about. She could tell I was hip to her tall tales because she would laugh like crazy at times. I wish I could hold a smile and laugh as much as she did because the divorce was getting ugly.

While I was in school, my daddy was in court fighting to retain custody of my younger siblings and me. I tried my best to do my schoolwork, but I always thought about what would happen to us. To add to my growing list of problems, this punk ass kid in my class tried to rank on me once.

"Bro, I'm not in the mood today. Can you stop please?" I tried to keep my cool, but he ignored my request.

"Thad, you sound like a bitch . . . like your mama while she was on my di——"

Before he could even finish the word, I swung with a mean ass right hook and knocked bro out of his desk. What the hell was he thinking talking to me like that? I asked him to stop, I gave him a chance, but he wanted to be stupid. So, I whopped his ass and showed him who was a bitch. He cried and begged me to stop as I planted my knuckles into his face. The whole class was lit up with "oooohhhh's" and yelling as the teacher tried to break up the squabble. The gym coach ran in to pull me off the kid and escorted us both to the principal's office. I felt good after beating the hell out of dude because it relieved me of all my frustrations for a moment.

"Mr. Tolbert, you seem to have a short temper and that will cause greater problems in the future." The principal spoke to me as if she was a psychologist or my mama.

Before I knew it, my eyes filled with tears and I could not hold on to them anymore. The principal grilled me to see why I was crying, but I just wiped my face and held my silence. Everyone knew the code at home: "What happens in my house stays in my house. Don't be out here making it seem like you are not being taken care of or that's your ass Mr. Postman!"

The principal called my mama and daddy to explain what had happened and that I was being suspended. I thought to myself, *if she only knew what I was going through, maybe she would understand my frustrations and why I am the way I am.* My parents were going at it in court at the time. I remained silent as she was unsuccessful at reaching them. That is until she assigned me to in school suspension (ISS) for the rest of the day.

The hallway filled with running kids as the school dismissal bell rang. I bolted out of the room when the principal yelled out, "And where are you going, sir? I'm walking with you to your dad's car today."

At that point, it was time to anchor down and brace myself for an ass whooping. My principal was dramatic as hell with her stories, so I already knew she was going to make it seem like I had declared war in the classroom that day.

"Good afternoon, Mr. Tolbert. I hate to be the bearer of bad news, but Thaddeus assaulted a student in class today and will be on suspension for three days."

Can you believe this lady? Not once did she mention this boy started shit with me and kept going after I asked him to stop. I noticed the look on my daddy's face and he was not trying to hear me out. Once the principal left, I tried to tell him what really happened and all he could say was, "When we get home, you already know what's about to happen, so don't get comfortable and don't do shit else but wait on me in my room."

That was the problem: instead of understanding why I had issued that beatdown, my daddy was ready to give me one of my own. I had no voice to say how messed up I thought that was, but it was either shut up and take the whooping or run off at the mouth and possibly catch the hands. I held my ground and took that belt. As I cried, I pictured my mama getting her ass beat. Mama Bea told me to pray, but I wondered why God never saved us from those beatdowns. I still believed no matter what and I still prayed night and day.

Soon Friday arrived—the last day of my suspension. As Mama Bea would say, my siblings and I were on the front porch getting some cool breeze. My daddy pulled up and something seemed strange about him that day. I did not hear any music as he pulled into the driveway and he sat in the car for a while before exiting. Before I fixed my mouth to greet him, he walked up the porch saying, "Y'all pack your things up . . . I can't believe they gave y'all to that bitch."

My heart sunk so low that it touched my confidence, or lack thereof. Everything I had ever known was gone and I really could not understand why. Things had been messed up for a long time because all everyone would do was curse, argue and criticize each other. I guess that was normal because that is how everyone in the ghetto speaks.

When the time came for us to move in with our mama, I found myself filled with bittersweet emotions. I was glad that we would be with Mama, but I was hurt because we would be leaving my daddy. The court deemed daddy highly abusive, so the court ordered supervised visits with Mama Bea being present. Daddy always told me that the courts always sided with the woman and slapped a label on the black man. I guess he was not lying after all. Yes, my daddy kicked ass, but I know he loved Mama and I damn sure know that he loved us. Regardless, I knew I would not like the change one bit. I could see the hurt in my daddy's eyes and all I could do was cry.

As we loaded the car with our things, I could not help but think about all the good and bad times. I really did not want to leave the only place I had ever known. All I knew was 2509; all I knew was 3rd Ward, the ghetto. I cried harder as we said our goodbyes to Daddy, Uncle Greg, my aunt and Mama Bea.

Daddy hugged me tight as he whispered, "Always be strong and stand your ground. I love you."

From there we piled into the car and drove off into the sunset. I thought maybe we all needed that experience to realize some things needed to change in our family. At least we would be free from those beatdowns. I decided to give this new life a shot and see how things would go.

We pulled up to some apartments called Forum Plaza on Forum Park. We were all the way on the southwest side of town and I did not know a damn thing about this place. All my boys were back in the hood, no more EP, and I could not see my daddy nor Mama Bea when I wanted to. This shit hurt and I wished Mama and Daddy could feel my pain.

After unpacking and lying down for the night, I could not really sleep because the tears would not stop falling. I missed my daddy the way I missed my mama when she left us in the hood. *I know they love us, but do they really care? This pain I feel inside is like no other and it's cold as hell in here. The A/C is good, but my heart is not. I wonder if this is what Lance's people felt like before he took his last breath.* I wondered what the hell did I know about dying besides seeing the yellow homicide tape, watching the news, and hearing stories at the lunch table. I knew enough not to want it knocking at my door. I knew enough not to want it to go down when I saw Daddy choking Mama. I knew enough not to want it on Uncle Greg as Daddy choked him because he could not handle his words. I knew enough not to want it on myself as Daddy pushed my head against the wall and choked me. I often thought, *take me now God . . . save me from this cold world because I don't want to feel this shit anymore*. I wanted to die, but all I could do was pray for things to get better. Only this time I did not fall asleep; I lied awake until sunrise staring at the ceiling.

Mama made us breakfast as we watched "One Saturday Morning" cartoons. Taylor, Lawrence and I just chilled on the sofa like we always did. No matter what happened, we always had each other. The last thing I wanted to see was anything happening to them or to anyone in my family. Mama joined us and told us how we were going to go out and do things as a family. *How can we do that and Daddy is not here?* I just went along with the flow and enjoyed the moment. I could tell something was up with Mama, but she never revealed much of herself until she reached her breaking point—I inherited those ways from her. Nevertheless, it was a good day and we sealed it off with dinner and movies. Before I knew it, I was knocked out cold on the couch. Not sleeping the night before had finally caught up to me.

The next morning, I heard Mama's voice in my ear telling me to wake up. *Damn, I haven't heard that in a good while and it really feels great.* As I brushed my teeth, Mama peeped her head in the bathroom saying, "Thadd, pack a bag and be ready in a few minutes."

Sunday's were normally a chill day, but that day was a different story. We loaded up in the car and headed up 59 North. Once we started following a certain route, I immediately knew where we were headed—3rd Ward! We eventually pulled up to our house and Mama Bea greeted us on the front porch. We sat down with her as Mama went inside to talk to Daddy. My nosey ass went to eavesdrop but pretended like I was using the restroom.

"I don't like the way they did you in court. I can't see myself keeping them away from you and Mama like that."

Mama initiated the conversation about us with Daddy. Daddy responded, "You know I will take care of them, no doubt, and they can stay but if we're going to do this, we're going to play by my rules." I sat on the toilet hell of excited from a conversation I had no business listening to.

Trying to hide my excitement, I was happy just thinking about walking into the next room to see Uncle Greg, Mama Bea or my daddy, but I really wished Mama could stay with us. Just the thought of it saddened me. However, we would still get to see her every morning before school and on weekends. It seemed like we were on a good path with this new agreement because we got to see both of our parents. It just sucked that Mama Bea's health started to decline at the time. *I hope we can all get our shit together and be the family we once were.*

CHAPTER 4
SOUL FOOD

At twelve years old, I found myself in the kitchen whipping up a mean ass dinner with Mama Bea—some good smothered pork chops, greens, candied yams, rice and corn bread. I had to keep an eye out because she was on a special diet due to her being on dialysis, and you know how folks get around pots in the kitchen—always wanting a sample before dinner is ready.

I went to the restroom and returned not even two minutes later to find Mama Bea in the pot of greens. "Mama, what are you doing in that pot?"

I startled her and she could not do anything but laugh. "I'm just having a lil' taste . . . the doctor said I can have just a lil' taste."

Mama Bea knew damn well that was not a taste she had just scarfed down, but I could only laugh right along with her. Beau Jocque's "Motor Dude Special" started playing on her radio, so we could not help but Zydeco all over the kitchen.

Mama Bea hollered out, "Ayyyeee me ye sha . . . go on and boogaloo!" Boy, that French Creole accent can strike you at any given moment. We damn near forgot that we were cooking until we started smelling the aroma of that good corn bread seeping through the oven door. It was time for us to enjoy the good old eating we had prepared.

I could not help but think about some of my homeboys from the hood wondering if they were eating as good as I was. We were now at different schools—they attended Ryan and I attended Lanier—and I still saw them quite often in the hood, but some things had changed since elementary school. I had been hearing stories about how some of their mothers either left them hanging with their grandmothers or sold all their furniture for crack. One day my boy Josh walked up to Mama Bea and me as we walked to the corner store. He damn near had tears in his eyes asking us for noodles so that he and his younger siblings could eat that night. I almost cried for him. Things at my house were not peachy keen, but Daddy and Mama Bea made sure we ate every night. I had my people for the most part, but thinking about my boys and their siblings being abandoned made me appreciate what I had even more. Hell, if I was going to Ryan, I would have taken them a few plates just to make sure they were good. You just never knew in my ghetto.

Once all the dishes were washed and put away and everyone had bathed and brushed their teeth, it was time to watch television with Mama Bea and Uncle Greg until the news came on; that is how we knew it was time for us to head to bed. We would always try to stay up past 9 p.m. but would scatter like roaches whenever we heard my daddy's room door open.

"In breaking news, and IED went off in Baghdad, Iraq as an American convoy passed through the street today, killing everyone on board, including two from the Houston, Texas area and injuring several other civilians."

It seemed like someone died every day fighting that war overseas, but I wondered if they would ever show the war zone within walking distance of my house. I guess it is true what Doughboy said on *Boyz N the Hood*, "Either they don't know, don't show, or don't care about what's going on in the hood." It was not all that bad, but it was not all that good either. I thought maybe God would see it and help us if they broadcasted the ghetto. *Mama Bea said God is always watching and working, so we should never question him. Well when I see him, we must have a long talk! Until then, I'm peeping my surroundings because something doesn't feel right.*

Things suddenly seemed different in our house one day. It was Mother's Day Sunday, but Daddy was the only one in the kitchen cooking. It did not matter what day of the week it was or what was going on—Mama Bea never skipped a beat in the kitchen. She also did not sleep past 7 a.m. and even if she took a midday nap, it never lasted longer than an hour. I do not recall her being around the house much that day, which was strange. I did not pay it much attention, though, as I made her and my mama a Mother's Day Card.

I traced a lion from one of Taylor's books that gave instructions on how to draw animals. I was into poetry and theatre arts at the time, so I sat still as I pondered my message. I thought about my daddy whipping up some fried chicken, mashed potatoes, green peas and macaroni and cheese. That is when it hit me. I began to write, "You're brave as a lion. I smell the chicken fryin' . . . I'll put it on a tray. Happy Mother's Day!" I know that shit is lame, but damn I tried.

Later I walked into Mama Bea's room to wake her up because the family was on the way to eat and celebrate. It was not hard to wake her up; just get near her and she would jump out of the bed and damn near out of her moo moo. This time was a different story, though.

She took her time sitting up and began to talk funny. "Hey sha, are we home yet?"

I gave her a puzzled look because we had not gone anywhere. "Mama, what are you talking about? We are home." I was so confused as she continued to look at me the same way.

"No, we're supposed to go home . . . Selena, Mama Lena and them said they're coming to get me."

This scared me a little because everyone she named was deceased. Selena was her younger sister and she had died the year before. I remembered her funeral like it was yesterday—it was my very first.

The family began to arrive, so we left the room to greet them. Even as I greeted everyone with smiles and hugs, I just could not stop thinking about what Mama Bea had said.

Later that day we sat around the living room eating, laughing and jamming to the radio. Uncle Greg is the family's comedian, so it was expected for everyone to be crying laughing at whatever came out of his mouth. During all the laughter, I could not help but notice Mama Bea breathing extra hard as she tried to participate in the festivities. My older cousin must have seen the concerned look on my face because she looked just as puzzled as I did while asking Mama Bea if she was alright. The music continued playing in the background, but the house went dead silent as the attention shifted to Mama Bea.

"Yeah, baby, I'm alright; just a little tired."

She had been sleeping damn near all day, so I knew she was just putting on a front for us not to worry. My cousin asked her if she wanted to go to the hospital but in her typical stubbornness, she said, "Hell no." Everyone continued with their previous conversations as I sat there thinking about Mama. I started thinking to myself, *this feels like the scene on the movie Soul Food when Big Mama Jo refused to get her leg amputated. I'm now looking at things through Ahmad's eyes.* I then laughed with the rest of the family as Uncle Greg roasted on one of my cousins. Sometimes you had to laugh to keep from crying in my house. You could not let anyone see you in your feelings.

A few days later, I found myself working on an assignment to close out the school year. I could not help but think about how I was entering my last year of middle school and how I was becoming serious about playing football. It was a peaceful evening in my ghetto as the sun set beautifully in the west. I said to myself, *God is good. Mama Bea always told me to have Faith. I guess this is what Faith feels like.*

"Mama, what's wrong? Are you alright?" I heard my cousin's voice coming from Mama Bea's room.

I walked in to find her lying in bed breathing extra hard again. My cousin helped her drink from a cup of water.

She caught her breath just enough to say, "Okay . . . I'm ready to go now."

Now frantic as hell, I ran to get the phone to call 911. I took deep breaths to keep myself calm because I had experienced this before. Between Uncle Greg's seizures and Mama Bea suffering from heart failure twice, I knew things would be okay. They were always okay. The paramedics rushed into the house and loaded Mama Bea onto the stretcher. Taylor stood in the doorway crying, so I rushed over to console my little sister.

"It's going to be okay," I told her. "Mama is in God's hands and He will make her feel better." Inside, I was crying, too, but as her big brother, I held it together to show her the strength Mama Bea had instilled in us all.

As the ambulance drove away in the direction of St. Joseph Medical Center, a tear flowed down my cheek. I could see myself chasing the ambulance with Mama Bea reaching out to me, but I could not keep up with it and soon it was too far for me to see. In reality, my daddy was grabbing me by the shoulders telling me it would be alright.

He sure does know how to hold things together at crazy times.

Daddy and my Aunt Loyce jumped in his car to make their way to the hospital so that they could be there when the doctor returned with his findings. I wondered if Daddy could help fill the empty feeling in the house when he came home.

On the last day of school, my boys and I were live in the gym, listening to music, signing yearbooks and pulling girls' numbers. My boy Will grabbed me by my shoulders. "Damn, Thadd, bro . . . we're about to be in the 8th grade like a motherfucker!"

I laughed hard as I hugged my dog back. Will was from 3rd Ward, too, so he knew the deal. Through my ups and many downs, I knew I could count on my bro Will to be in my corner. He even prayed with me in person and on the phone at night. He prayed that Mama Bea would make it back home so that we could cook that good soul food. Mama said she was going to make me a peach cobbler for my birthday. Though it was only May and my birthday was in September, I did not give a damn.

After school I caught the 82 Westheimer bus on my way to the Pierce Elevation to catch the 52 Scott bus. It would drop me off right by the house on McGowen and Hutchins. Instead of going home, I walked to St. Joseph to see Mama Bea in the ICU. The doctor said she had another kidney failure and her blood pressure had been too low to do her dialysis treatment. Though this weakened her heart, Mama Bea was a fighter. I just knew she would be ready to come home before the month was over.

"Hey, Mama, how are you today sha?" I put my backpack down by her bedside and sat in the chair next to her bed. It was quiet as a mouse in there, but you could hear the beeps of the heart monitor. Mama Bea looked more tired than the last time I saw her. It must have been a constant battle in there and I knew she could not wait to go home.

"I'm going to the 8th grade now. The coach even said I'm getting better at football." I continued giving her the latest scoop even though she could not respond. "Taylor, Lawrence, Daddy and Greg are doing fine as well. We all miss you, baby, and we can't wait for you to come home."

I grabbed her hand and a tear hit my cheek once again. As I wiped my face, I felt her grip my hand. I gripped her a bit tighter before I leaned over to kiss her cheek. "I'll be back to see you soon sha." I picked up my backpack and walked out the room headed toward the nearest bus stop.

I finally arrived home fifteen minutes later, much later than my expected time to be home.

"Boy, where in the fuck have you been?" Daddy greeted me at the front porch with a stern and pissed off look on his face.

"Sorry I'm late, but the bus took a long time to come." He knew I was lying, so he slapped me upside my head.

"Lie to me again! Three buses done passed by here and you were not on any of them . . . Why?" I broke down crying and told him I went to see Mama Bea. I missed the hell out of my granny and that mean ass headache was not making it any better.

"Got dammit, boy! Next time tell me where you are instead of having me worry to death. It's enough going on as is."

I replied, "Yes sir," as I walked into the house rubbing my head.

We experienced another Sunday at home without Mama Bea. We had just finished cleaning up a few buildings with Daddy. That is how we paid the bills—cleaning office buildings through the janitorial business Daddy had opened the year before. Lord knows I hated spending late nights and weekends cleaning buildings, but it was cool seeing something you owned with your name on it: Tolbert Unlimited. Daddy said he wanted to leave something for us to own long after he left his shell behind in the cold world.

"Our job is not done, though; we still have to paint the front porch." Daddy jokingly but seriously gave me a heads-up not to get comfortable when we got home. Soon it was time to unload the truck and get ready for some more work.

Somehow, I was always stuck doing the dirty work with Daddy while Taylor and Lawrence chilled in the house. I never questioned his authority, though, because I refused to get slapped upside the head. We were working hard headed from the entryway of the front door to the lounge area of the porch when Daddy received a call from my cousins and aunt at the hospital. Mama Bea was in her hospital room laughing and talking up a storm. That was the best news I had heard in a while. It looked like my prayers had been answered and Mama Bea would be coming home right on time.

"How's Thadd, Taylor and Lawrence?" I heard my baby's voice over the phone and a Kool-Aid smile spread across my face. *Looks like we'll be getting that soul food back on our plates soon.*

Memorial Day was a dreary day that year, so we had to play inside. Daddy helped Taylor and I download the Math Blaster computer game, but the DSL seemed to be tripping that day. The house phone then rang interrupting the internet connection. It was my cousin calling from the hospital and she wanted to talk to Daddy. She sounded kind of worried, but I paid it no mind as I passed him the phone. Shortly after he hung up the phone and continued to help us with the game. Twenty minutes later, my cousin called again but this time his face changed drastically.

"I'll be back y'all and Thadd, keep an eye on your brother and sister."

Taylor and I continued to play the game as we waited for Mama to come over. We were going to see Mama Bea that day, and I was so excited to see her. Mama walked in the door and Taylor went to get her hair box so that Mama could comb her hair. I shut the computer down and began to get dressed as well.

As I put on my shoes, I noticed people started to pull up to the house one by one. My aunt walked in with a case of Miller Lite and my cousins followed her. *Damn, all of this must mean Mama Bea is coming home.* Daddy finally returned and went into his room to use the bathroom. I became excited and started helping Lawrence get ready.

My aunt and my cousin walked into my room. "What y'all in here doing?"

As I tied Lawrence's shoes, I responded, "I'm getting Lawrence ready so we can go see Mama Bea." When I stood up, I noticed the sad look on their faces.

My cousin looked at my aunt and said, "I'll tell him . . . Mama died."

Tears started pouring from her eyes as the oxygen left the room. I gasped for air as a waterfall of tears poured down my face. My cousin Adriene hugged me tight to console me, but I could not find the energy to hug her back. I hurried to Mama Bea's room where I found Taylor and my mama. I tried to gather myself, but I noticed people on the porch bawling.

I entered the room and my mama stared at me. "Boy, what's wrong with you?" I took a deep breath and cried out, "Mama Bea died!"

My mama stopped plaiting Taylor's hair, frozen with her mouth open. Taylor let out a loud cry and Mama reached out to hug us both.

I can't believe this . . . she's really gone. Daddy always told us that we all must leave this shell of ours behind one day and go to the kingdom with God. I just did not know this was how it was going to be or feel. The house already felt empty, but now it was even emptier. *Who's going to give me pocket change to go to the corner store? Who's going to be here to tell us stories about our family? Who's going to save us from Daddy when he goes overboard with his physical discipline?*

As nightfall arrived, I noticed shadows on Mama Bea's wall as I sat in the living room with Uncle Greg. My aunt and cousins were sorting through Mama Bea's things.

I guess they could not wait to get their hands on the few good things she left behind. I sat there hurt thinking, *Damn . . . this is my family; this is what Mama Bea left us with.*

I cried all I could cry that day and night. I laid my head down that night praying to God and asking a million and one questions though Mama Bea told me I should never question Him. *God, why couldn't you bring Mama Bea home like I asked you to? Never once thought it was time for Selena or Mama Lena to come get her and take her home with them. Now what's going to happen? When will this pain in my chest go away?* That night I questioned Faith as if it was another Louisiana folk tale.

After a while I closed my eyes and saw Mama Bea's face. I saw her wiping my tears. I felt her gripping my hand. When I opened my eyes, I could not see her anymore. I'm lost as hell right now God. *Damn, I have one more question for you; whatever happened to the soul food?*

CHAPTER 5
COLD NIGHTS WITH NO LIGHTS

Black suit, white shirt, black tie and black shoes. I stood in the mirror preparing myself to say "see you later" to Mama Bea. It was a hell of a morning in my house as the family gathered to ride to the funeral home together. My emotions were all over the place, but I tried to be strong like my daddy. I had yet to see him drop one tear. There he was, Mama Bea's youngest, holding everything and everyone together as she would.

The family car pulled up in front of the house and Daddy began to rally everyone up. No lie, I felt hell of butterflies in my stomach at that moment. I walked with Uncle Greg to the car and whispered to him, "Man, I gotta hit this bathroom ASAP!" His laugh made the urge and the butterflies disappear. Once in the limo, I glanced at everyone's face and could clearly see that I was not the only one who thought they had to go.

We drove off and a long line of cars followed. I looked around the ghetto thinking about those many walks Mama Bea and I took down McGowen. I wish I could feel her gripping my hand like she used to do as we walked across the street. I realized we take so many things for granted and often do not realize it until those things are taken from us. I wondered if Lance felt the same thing when he had to say see you later to his people. Man, my mind raced like crazy. *Damn, there goes my heart too.*

As we reached our destination, I noticed the hearse parked in the driveway of the funeral home. *Damn, I don't think I'm ready for this. Can my heart really stand to see Mama like this?* I thought back to the many talks my daddy gave us to prepare us for this day. Regardless of what anyone says, no one can be adequately prepared to see that open casket at the pulpit.

I walked with Uncle Greg into the chapel to view the body and my heart sank as we neared the casket. She appeared to be sleeping peacefully in her favorite maroon church suit. I wondered how Uncle Greg felt because he never showed his emotions unless he was pissed. I helped him sit down on the front row then walked outside to march in with the rest of the family.

My aunt walked in first with my daddy as she is the oldest and he is the baby boy. She kissed Mama's cheek and Daddy followed her lead. All my cousins kissed her cheek, too. Mama and Taylor approached with tears in their eyes. I rubbed Mama Bea's arm thinking, *I guess this is it.* I kissed her on her cheek one last time and took a deep breath as a tear fell on her cheek. I wiped the tears from Taylor's eyes and sat down next to my cousins.

Once the whole family had been seated, the funeral director began to close the lid. All the oxygen left the room and my vision became blurry. The tears poured down my face and my cousin hugged me tight. I finally caught my breath and exhaled deeply. The service continued as my cousins roasted on what people wore to the funeral. I found myself crying laughing at this point. When my other aunt started singing, the laughs disappeared, and my heart grew heavier. I had never lost anyone I was close to, so the pain was excruciating.

My thoughts raced again as the pallbearers carried the casket to the hearse. I thought about my daddy's strength because he was among the six pallbearers. I tried to keep my composure as we followed them outside. We all entered the car and rode in silence to the gravesite. *To Paradise we go as we take that last ride with Mama Bea down Martin Luther King, Jr.*

That long drive down the row came to an end and we found ourselves seated in front of the casket. My mama hugged me tight as the tears rained down during the preacher's committal sermon.

May you be healed, comforted and sustained. May the Father, by his grace, grant you forgiveness, mercy and comfort. May he enfold you within your fellowship of love and in the household of faith. May he enlighten you in your seeking. May he deepen your sense of trust. I pray that he will unravel your mixed up, confused feelings so that you may face what you must in a triumphant way, through Christ Jesus. Amen.

I tried to hold on to my Faith, but it was hard to after what I had just experienced. I hung my head low as we walked back to the car.

A family friend grabbed me by the shoulder. "Hold your head up high, Thadd . . . there is no reason to hang your head for she remains with you."

I honestly was not trying to hear all that, but I picked my head up anyway. Staring at Mama Bea's casket through the car window, I thought, *Damn, we are really leaving her here. Daddy always said one day we will leave this old shell behind and live on in spirit. Spirit if you hear me, please mend this broken heart!*

We slowly drove away from the cemetery as I told Mama goodbye in my head. I wanted to cry, but no more tears would fall. I felt confused, lost, hurt, in disbelief, broken and pissed off. *God, you really let me down. Mama, why did you leave me? You always told me to have Faith, but how can I do that right now? Why do I want to scream, but you won't let me open my mouth? Lord, why am I getting cold?* As we left the cemetery and turned onto Cullen, I left that lady named Faith right where we left my Mama Bea.

I soon found myself cleaning buildings with Daddy again, but I was not feeling this shit anymore. It was late and I still had homework to do. Luckily, we were on the last building and ready to close shop. We then hit the 90 to 59 North to head back to the hood. Daddy bumped the Smooth Jazz 95.7 The Wave station, which made me sleepy as hell. *To do my homework or not? Fuck it, I can get up early with Mama Bea to do it.* Then reality sank in; it had been five months and I was still adjusting to my grandmother being gone.

We pulled up to the house and it seemed extra dark on my row. We normally saw Uncle Greg's television on in the living room, but I figured he went to bed early. I walked in and clicked the hallway light . . . nothing! CenterPoint had caught us slipping and turned the lights off. *If it's not one thing, it's another.* The gas had been turned off shortly before and we had been hustling with Daddy to keep things going. However, we knew how to maneuver around the house in the dark because we did not have many lights anyway.

After Taylor and Lawrence had washed up for dinner, I followed behind them to take a cold wash off in Daddy's bathroom sink. It was already cold, so I was freezing my balls off in there. For dinner we ate ham and cheese sandwiches with chips and were full like we had eaten soul food. I wanted to do my homework but because we did not have any lights, I figured the homework could wait.

I really wished Mama Bea was there to make everything better. I was told God gives his strongest warriors the hardest wars. So, I guess there was a point to this struggle, but I did not want Faith coming anywhere near me because she had already let me down before. I had not prayed since the funeral and I did not plan on doing it anytime soon. *I wonder if He's even listening to me or seeing what we are going through? If so, how can He let us struggle like this?* I was supposed to be focused on school and football, but helping my daddy with my younger siblings and Uncle Greg made me feel as if I was facing grown man problems.

"Big Thadd, what's good, man . . . how you are holding up?" My bro Z ran up to me in the hallway as I walked to class one day.

"I'm good bro . . . trying to maintain and get through this shit."

Z was from 3rd Ward as well so he understood the struggle. In fact, his mama and my cousin Stew were best friends; you can say we were more like family than friends. I could tell bro anything without him judging me. We sat down in class and talked about that ghetto life. Other students pulled up a chair as I poured out my soul.

Just the other day, the lights were turned off in broad daylight while we were at home. Daddy just went grocery shopping and stocked up on meat and perishables, so we ran an extension cord from the neighbor's house to have the fans, refrigerator and freezer running. Daddy was ashamed that we had to do that and he held us crying that night.

Z understood what I was going through, but many of our classmates could not wrap their minds around it. Lanier is near River Oaks, West University and Bellaire, so many of our classmates' parents had that bank, driving

Porsche, Benz and Lexus. They lived in those big houses with the curved driveway; they lived the American dream without a care in the world. That was cool because we appreciated the little that we had though we had ghetto dreams about more. Some of us had our own beds and bedroom at home; some of us slept at the trap house or shelter, but we did not complain and went to school every day like nothing was even fucked up at home.

I soon heard some of my boys were out there getting it to eat. Twelve and thirteen-year-olds jumped off the porch to see what that life was about. Some of the guys jumped down with blue; some flaming red. My big bro was a Blood and I saw my cousin and patnas doing their thing, too; so, I stepped off just to experience it for myself.

Going to school on the south Westside meant one thing—we had to see the Cholos. Every other day we fought in the restroom and hulled them boys out. One day

Z left one of them leaking in a puddle of his own blood. I know they did not like that, but it is what it is. After this incident they waged war against us when they jumped bro in the restroom. They really messed up jumping one of ours. HISD police was ready and let it be known that they had the paddy wagon ready for anyone who fought on school grounds. We did not take heed to that warning and proceeded to whoop on some Cholos. The officers chased some of us but could not catch anyone.

I ran to wait for my bus at the stop. One of the older Cholos came out of nowhere to charge me up. I was not scared to fight anyone, so he pulled out a blade like that was going to faze me. Before I could make my move, my boy hurdled over the trash can by the bus stop and hit the dude with a mean ass right jab to the jaw. I promise dude went to sleep right on Westheimer.

Z got expelled later that week. He was on his way to alternative school and I was following in his footsteps. Giving me a much-needed reality check, he told me to chill and not to let those haters block my shine. My brother always knew what to say. I promise he helped me get through those cold nights with no lights. If he only knew how much those words meant to me during that torrential storm.

Every day I dealt with people who did not understand my struggle and could care less about my well-being. I was born into those circumstances; I did not ask to be here. I did not create my narrative; it was written for me prior to my existence. All I could do was keep my cool and make my moves as quietly as possible. I just could not wait until those nights were over.

CHAPTER 6
THE LION'S DEN

Now back on my side of town walking down the legendary hallways that Big Moe, Phylicia Rashad, Debbie Allen, Michael Young and many more legends have walked, I thought of myself as JY fly. As the 3rd generation of my family to walk these halls, I had some major shoes to fill. I promise it felt good to see so many familiar faces.

I often chilled in this one class not caring what the teacher talked about. All she did was talk down to us and compare us to the students in the movie *Lean on Me* before Dr. Clark took over. Hell, she even played the movie a few times like it was supposed to move us. I wondered, *what in the hell does this have to do with the class? Is this going to be on the TAKS test as well? Seems like that's the only thing that matters around here.* However, it seemed like the TAKS test was designed for us to fail. I had never failed the test, but I hated the look on some of my homeboys' faces when those results came in. It was a constant struggle to get by, even in education.

"Aye, ho ass nigga . . . what's that shit you was talking?" Some rumbling emerged from the hallway and now every classroom on the floor was in the hall spectating the fight. "Whooooooppp! Get y'all ass back in class right now!" Mr. White flared the siren on his bullhorn. He seemed to be everywhere like clockwork with that bullhorn.

No one moved until the school police came running through. Can you imagine over 100 people running down a narrow hallway? You would have thought the jumpers had hopped out on us. Anything was bound to happen at The Yard on campus or off.

As we left campus to go home, we noticed some boys running like crazy in the direction of Cuney Homes. I could tell they were trying to avoid a beatdown. There are certain places in 3rd Ward you do not go if you are not known or if you are deemed sweet—The Bricks is one of those places. You could not get caught slipping on D-Block or the Backline because if you did, someone would find out at school and get on your ass even more.

I continued walking to the 52 Scott bus stop to head back to Dodge City. I was supposed to be at football practice, but my insurance waiver had not cleared yet. The state programs would always be slow with your shit but would be on your ass if you took your time on their time. *Oh well, I'll just hit the house and knock out this homework.* I kid you not, as the bus took off, I noticed someone getting jumped at the bus stop across the street. Those boys took off with bro's new Jordan. Like I said before, it was bound to go down anywhere on or off campus at The Yard.

As the bus turned off Scott on to McGowen, I eyed several of my peers from school getting to it. My palms itched to get to it, too, but the last thing I needed was my daddy and nosey family all in my mix for hitting licks. It was already a crime to them that I had a few hundred dollars on me at a time. No need to go into the details about how I got it, just know I got it.

Being broke and unable to make ends meet is not a game you want to play. This makes it difficult for a kid to walk the straight and narrow even though he knows he should. You get tired of your parents or guardians telling you no, and you learn survival tactics from not having your basic needs met. It is either stack or starve, wait on something or take something.

I empathized with the boys that ran up on bro at the bus stop. I even felt sorry for bro because he did not do anything to deserve getting jacked. Every day I faced a constant battle in my mind about doing the right thing versus following the trend. My thoughts drifted back to my reality as I made it home. I had to knock out my homework before going to clean those weak ass buildings with Daddy.

Time is money and if you waste time, you lose money in the process. It seemed as if I was mopping those floors to help keep the lights, and whatever else, from being turned off. No lie, I really needed money at the time. In every office I vacuumed, I searched for money or something I could put in my pockets to make my itchy palms go away. The owner of this company was a hunter so I was even looking for his tools, but all I could find was the ammunition. *Hell, that will do for now . . . I can sell these rounds for the low. I'm going to make being dragged into these buildings*

worth my while one way or another.

I knew a few dudes that packed their tools to school. That should let you know how crazy it got there, being fourteen and older worrying about packing a tool just to make it home. One day, there was a shooting in the bricks over a dice game. I had met bro a few times at the blue store and it was crazy to see him go. It was nothing new to us, though; something was bound to happen on our side of town. It seemed crazy to me how the media referred to 3rd Ward as 3rd Ward when a murder or drug bust occurred but referred to it as Midtown any other time. They might as well have called us nigga right to our faces to show us how they really felt. Again, like Doughboy said, "Either they don't know, don't show, or don't care about what's going on in the hood." I took that scene to heart. The blues we speak of in the hood often goes unheard. I figured the people elected to represent us were just like Faith, only coming around when it was convenient. I just knew one thing: I was tired of being broke.

With so much going on in my mind, so much on my plate for a young soul, my only worry should have been school and football. I was always told to stay in my place and to enjoy being young while I can, but the grown-up problems I had been handed had me in a frenzy. I had to take it, though, because an ounce of complaining or crying about the situation would not fix anything. It would be minimized and pushed to the back burner.

Feelings could not be expressed in my house unless you paid bills and had mouths to feed. I bottled that shit up instead and put it to the back of my mind the best way I could. *This can't be living, and you can't tell me it is. How do they expect me to keep my head on straight and not wild out in these conditions? I'm over my shoulders in walking these streets and at home because some bullshit seems to be always lurking. It is what it is because in a few more years, I'll be away from this madness. Where will I be? Hell, I don't know as of right now. Hopefully in college playing ball or something but the way the ghetto is setup and according to the people, I'll be in the pen like my cousins or dead. No lie, that last part doesn't sound so bad right now. It seems like that's the only time people even claim to love you. At least then I'd get to be back with Mama Bea just like old times. Pac said, "Death gotta be easy 'cause life is hard. It's a shame to be this emotionally scarred." That's what happens when you force someone who is seeking direction to bottle up their thoughts and feelings and walk on eggshells. I can't be the only one with this problem. Oh well, I'll just fire up and smoke my pain away.*

One night I attempted to boil a large pot of water for a warm bath, but there was one problem—the hot plate shorted out and all the stores were closed. Because the gas was off, eliminating the stove as an option, I could either take a cold bath or throw a big popcorn bowl of water in the microwave. I could not stand a cold bath, so I chose the microwave. This is where those survival tactics kick in and you make do with what you have. My parents always told us to be grateful because there was someone out there who would be thankful for the things we had. However, I would not even wish this type of struggle on my worst enemy. I dreaded the winter because it was going to be hell sleeping in that cold house. I know my other family members saw us going through the struggle, but they wanted to stunt on us and look the other way. I refused to trip on it. I used it as more fuel for the fire inside of me instead.

You must have heart to survive in the Lion's den. Any sign of weakness will get you preyed on. These conditions caged us in and trapped us. If you corner or abuse an animal, a completely different standard of living kicks in. Such survival tactics then become an opposition to American social norms. In the Lion's den, we lived by our own norms by any means. If I had to sell drugs to my people, then so be it. If I had to rob my brother just to have the things I lacked, then so be it. If I had to rake leaves, wash cars or get my hands dirty, then so be it. I guess my daddy tried to show me these things as we cleaned those buildings every day. I know he meant well and wanted the best for me, but I could not dig that lifestyle. I was living but did not feel alive. *Faith, if you can hear me, please send help. Sincerely, a broken heart and lost soul.*

As the seasons passed, my classes at school became slimmer. Many of my friends said to hell with the straight and narrow and joined the streets full-time. I felt those boys' pain, which made it even worse. How could we focus on doing the right thing when nothing, but bad things came our way? The blues tells a story of struggle, misery and pain. Its melody had become so familiar that the shit eventually played out. The crazy thing about it? I still had some hope left in me. *I'll keep my head in these books and holler at you boys later. I pray y'all be safe and make it back home to the people who love you. Even if no one is there to tell you that, I love you.* It was important to tell the brothers and sisters you grew up with that you loved them after every conversation because you never knew if they would make it back home after a long day in the ghetto.

"Off duty police officer shot and killed a man today after an attempted robbery."

Hard times truly called for drastic measures. I could only imagine what his last thoughts were. *Did he tell his family that he loves them? Did he get to kiss his mama before leaving the house? Was it really that bad to run up on someone who turned out to be a cop? Was this another attempt to exterminate my people?* I had so many questions that needed answers. Hell, I questioned the validity of everything during those days; you could never be too sure about anything. *If we truly have an equal opportunity out here, then why are we caught up in messed up situations? They got us trapped in this corner.*

The shooting became the talk of the school and it hit home even more. That cop gunned down my teammate's brother. I could not even imagine getting a call that my brother would not be coming home anymore. No more talks on the phone. No more movie nights. No more pick-up basketball or football games. No more laughing together during hard times. *Rest easy, King, you don't' have to deal with this strain and broken windows.*

During this tragedy, I also considered my own fate. *Stack or starve; wait on something or take something. Take your pick and pick well because either way, you must be prepared to deal with the consequences. I feel trapped without a sense of direction. There is no one to seek for the right answer, so I must go headfirst and hope for* the best. If I don't make it, I'm sorry, Mama, for breaking your heart. I'm sorry, Daddy, for not being the man you raised me to be. I'm sorry my brothers and sister for I have failed you all. I'm sorry ghetto for being added to an unwanted statistic. I was born to be a king, but I let my circumstances strip me of my crown. I knew better, but I chose to be a bad man. I'm a troubled young man trying to win the game with an unfair hand. I was playing to win the grand prize, but I fell short for a cheap cost. Don't worry, you are not facing anything we haven't seen before. Another case closed in front of my peers in the court of law, or funeral home. Don't lose hope though because you can be the change everyone talks about but do not have the courage to be. I fell for the trap, but you don't have to. You still have a chance to be that change. I hope you don't make the mistakes I've made, take the paths I've wandered, or miss the shots that I've taken but did not follow through with. Remember, it's all in the wrist, young brother.

I lied in my bed thinking about a note to self that had never been written but had always been on my mind. I dwelled on the consequences of past generations and the ones I must accept. As I closed my eyes, I prayed silently: *Dear Lord, I pray . . . please don't let me fall prey in the Lion's den.*

CHAPTER 7
CLASS OF '10

High school neared its end with major plans on the horizon. Football season was off to a good start, my grades were on point, and college seemed closer than ever. I still did not know where this road would lead, but I longed for a change of scenery. All I knew was the worse than good that 3rd Ward had to offer. Though it was not all that good or bad, my day ones made each day the absolute best. With CJ, Henry, Rashad, Ferunell, Keenan, Jon B. and Chance around, each day passed with ease. Shaquin and Charlise blessed every class with their voices from heaven. My cousin Don kept the boys on point with the latest cologne; he never wore the same scent twice.

The boys' basketball team captured the attention of people nationwide. It was a hell of a time to be at Jack Yates. Many legends and memories were made at The Yard and it was even more of an honor to wear my crimson and gold uniform week after week. Even my bros and I handled business on the football field, carrying on a tradition and chasing a state championship. For forty-eight minutes the lights shined bright on us as our families, friends and alumni roared loudly. As we dominated the opponent, all the trials, hardships and lessons from our environment no longer existed. It was only temporary because once we were back home without our armor, without the lights and without the cheers and praises, the game of life reminded us of the hand we had been dealt.

Natural support was non-existent in the hood. If someone talked about all the good you had done, someone else would point out how you were no better than he or she was and how you would not amount to anything because your family did not make it out. Even if you wanted out of the cycle, someone constantly reminded you of your family's curse. All the would've, could've, should've stories falsely became a part of your fate all because people from your row could not stand to see you make moves to get out of the bucket.

Where does that leave someone like me? Should I continue my mission or just follow in line because according to my environment, I was destined to fail and lose based on the hand I was dealt? I'll show you better than I can tell you. It's not my fault you squandered your life. It's not my fault you let this game take you over instead of allowing it to humble you to persevere. I have big plans and my bros are down with the come up. I refuse to fail and even if I fall short, I will find another way. So if you are worried about whether I feel like I am better than you, no I do not think that, but that is what makes me different and my own individual. If you are with it, vibe with it, but if you are not, respect my grind and mind. Now back to these moves.

As we continued to help my father clean buildings, I struggled to understand the lessons supposedly being taught to us. It seemed acceptable to put grown folks' problems on children's plates and call it teaching you to never work for anyone more than you must in life. I was not feeling this ideology at all, and the opportunity soon arrived for me to speak my mind. I was not worried about the consequences because I believed my daddy could not beat my ass any more than he already had.

"If you don't like it and can't follow my rules, go stay with your Mama because I'm not going to have a son that's bigger than me laying up on me."

So much for speaking my mind. Now I had to put cleaning buildings over my education and football. This made me want out even more; it made me want to grind even harder to break this messed up cycle. I did not know how much more I could take, though.

When playoffs time arrived, I knew grades would be coming out soon. Unfortunately, I was failing a class and on the verge of being ineligible to play. Because I was a student-athlete, my grades came before football. I made a judgment call to skip practice to go to tutorials to make up for the work I had missed; I would do everything in my power to be on the field with my brothers. I informed my position coach of my whereabouts so that it would not seem as if I was abandoning football, even though I believed favoritism affected my time on the field more than anything.

After writing for what seemed like forever, I finally increased my grade to 80% so that I could report back on the field with the team. Only one problem stopped me: my locker had been cleared of all my equipment. I was completely puzzled at this point. I admitted my mistake like a man, worked hard to fix that mistake, but it still was not good enough.

I received a poor excuse for an explanation.

"I understand that grades are important, but if you don't show up to practice, you won't play Jack Yates Football."

I said to hell with it and stormed out, eyes full of tears, heart filled with rage and anger, and mind on destruction. I cocked back to hit a brick wall when my brother Rashad grabbed me and hugged me as tight as he could. Love overpowered my hate as I hugged my bro back.

"It's going to be alright, Thaddo bro . . . Don't you give up on us because we refuse to give up on you. I don't care what you've been told, but you can do this . . . *we* can do this."

To know someone genuinely cares about and loves you can take you quite far. What's crazy is family should be the ones to get you over the hump and through the obstacles you face. I reflected on the love and support my former classmates received at home on the other side of town. Anything they wanted to do, they received the support they needed to do it. In my ghetto, you had to risk getting kicked out of the house just to voice your thoughts, feelings and passions. I once heard a friend's mom tell him either he pitched in with "the family business" or he had to get out of her house. That story sounded familiar. I think it is shameful that some of our black families put such pressure on their children so early in life.

That type of pressure makes you want to buck and do whatever the hell you want to do; sometimes it makes you want to hit the kill switch. *Maybe if they see me lying in a casket, they will understand these blues I write about. I was told you couldn't make it to heaven taking your own life, so I will smoke this hydro to ease this pain.* A few rotations in with my bro, I began to think: *what if the people who are stuck like zombies on water or that are spending their last on twenty rock felt or feels the way I feel right now? It seems like they are after something they will never reach. This is part of the cycle that keeps on repeating. I refuse to be stuck here and fall victim.*

We fell short of a state championship that year, but we were still on a mission. Some of the squad played basketball, some focused on college preparation, and some hit licks and ran the streets because they ran out of things to do. Seems like the only choices we had were to rob, hustle, shoot, hoop, ball or school. However, it was hard to focus on school with problems at home. As much as my palms itched, I focused on leaving this struggle behind me. That still did not stop me from selling pills while I washed cars and cut yards. Cleaning those buildings helped keep the lights on, but I needed something to add to the bread Uncle Greg broke with me. My daddy still tripped with me because he could smell that good Kush on me, and I was not trying to hear anything about cleaning buildings. I was just trying to graduate and bounce. Deep down I wished my daddy would help me make the right moves to go to college and play ball.

National Signing Day is near, and I found myself stuck with only one offer from Southern Nazarene University, an NAIA school in Oklahoma. I thought my grades and size were D1 quality, but I guess I had to be grateful. I signed my LOI and celebrated with my other bros that signed as well. What a feeling it was to have all this love around as we made moves to go to college. I always dreamed of playing for the University of Texas, Louisiana State University, Michigan State University and Alabama State University, but this would do for now. My hard work was paying off and I was showing the people that doubted me how much of a gift I am to this world. *I guess Faith is good after all.*

I still frequented the weight room to get stronger and more conditioned. I received an invite from SNU to watch the spring game and to explore what the program offered firsthand. My mama was hyped about the opportunity, so she planned the trip and we hit the road. I was amped and ready to show them what I could offer. I had never traveled outside of Texas other than to Lafayette, Louisiana, which was only twice when I was five and six, so this was a hell of an opportunity for my family and me.

During the drive, I closed my eyes to rest up for the next morning, but the sound of my phone ringing repeatedly disturbed my little nap.

Chance called me from back home in a panic. "Bro, they shot Stunna Bam at the party, bro!"

I could not believe the news. Stunna Bam was a cold little hustler from the bricks. He was like family in a sense because my cousin and his parents were in these streets together. *This cannot be happening.* I was in Dallas at the time and this disturbing news had me ready to say to hell with this trip. I needed to get back home to be with the fam. I thought about my bro Z because Stunna Bam was his little brother. Z was my brother, so his pain was my pain. To make matters worse, I stumbled across pictures of Bam with bloody bandages on his head on Facebook—a sight that I will carry to my grave with other sights I want to delete from my memory. An OG once told me, "Life is not a movie or show on TV. You can't pause it, yell cut or redo it. Once you make your move, it's made; once it's done, it's done."

May 1st, 2010 at 6:02 a.m., Jaylon "Stunna Bam" Calloway passed away, four days before his fifteenth birthday. This one hurt me, but I had a mission to carry out. I handled my business and watched my future team battle it out on the field. The whole time I thought about Bam Bam and how his life had been taken from him with no regard. I could not help but cry because the look in his eyes had been embedded in my brain—the type of trauma we experienced daily but could not talk about. *Don't worry Bam; they will hear our blues soon.*

When I returned the hood was quiet and beyond recognition. Not one smoker or D-Boy was in sight. No dogs barking, no gunshots going off, not even a siren ringing. It seemed like the whole Tre felt Bam's loss. I picked up a newspaper and recognized Ms. Michelle on the front page crying about her only son being stripped away from this world. The cold part about all of this? A mother crying over her baby is old news in the Tre. It is another part of the cycle that just keeps repeating itself.

Henry and I were on a roll on this wine wood tip. Prom season neared and we tried to get everything ready for the big night. We fulfilled liquor orders not giving a damn about being underage. This was the big time for us, so we were going to make the best out of it. Big bro blessed our game and it was going down.

On prom night, my daddy smelled that Kush cologne on me, and he did not like it at all, but that was the last thing on my mind. I was about to get fresh and party with the rest of the class of '10. Once we arrived lights flashed, music banged, and plenty of suited and dolled up people poured into the senior prom. CJ and I plotted going outside to put one in the air, but we joined the party in the middle of the dance floor instead. Rashad, Jiggin' Jo and other classmates posted up on the dance floor hyping everyone up. I loved seeing black people come together and enjoy themselves without any worries or drama.

As the night wound down, I stood on the balcony with my boys looking at the skyline thinking, *We're almost there.* CJ and I walked to the truck as everyone left prom to head to different after parties. We finally put one in rotation as we figured out the next move. We made a pit stop at Chance's hotel room before going to Rashad and Fernell's suite. That is where the party got real. It felt good to enjoy family without the B.S. I had to endure at home. Though I wanted the night to last forever, that was just wishful thinking.

Now back to reality, graduation was within reach. Because classes were basically over, it was smooth sailing from there. Senior trip, senior breakfast, then us walking across the stage. This was big for many of us because we were the first within our households to graduate from high school and to go to college.

Henry and I were still rolling and were inseparable at this stage in our life. One day we were riding home from school and talking about goals as usual. We pulled up to my house to find my daddy outside looking like he was about to talk shit.

"I done told your ass about hanging around these niggas like that. You're going to get into some shit you cannot get out of."

Always jumping to conclusions man . . . just can't win for losing in this house.

Later I noticed I left my graduation cap with my friend, so I called her and asked her to drop it off at my house. As she pulled off, my daddy was at it again, but only this time he ran up in my face calling me every name except the one he and my mama gave me. I was pissed off to the point that the man standing before me was not my father—I saw the old head I had knocked out on McGowen a few years prior. I saw all the times my father pulled me out of bed to beat, choke and abuse me over all the juice or soda being gone and other stupid shit. All the years of his bullshit I put up with was now at the front of my mind and I was waiting for him to make his move. He grabbed my neck and the beast in me snapped. Just when I was about to go in, my neighbor grabbed me and walked with me up the street to grab a soda and cool off. Never have I ever been so mad to the point that I was willing to take that risk and take my daddy to the grass. He always said that he would kill me before he let me beat his ass. I was content with someone leaving our house in a body bag that day, and it was not going to be me.

I returned home after an hour or so and sat in my backyard. Taylor came outside to console me and told me it was going to be okay. My daddy came outside still on that bullshit and told me that if I wanted to disrespect him like that, I should carry my ass on up the street like I wanted to be. I left with tears in my eyes and my little sister's cries in my ears. I wish Mama Bea were there to stop this shit, but I would rather be out on the streets than to be in that hell hole another day.

I sat at the bus stop most of the night thinking about my life's meaning. *What is my purpose and why am I still here?* Once I ran out of questions, I began to fall asleep.

"Thaddo bro, what you are doing, bro?"

I heard a familiar voice coming from a car that had stopped in front of me. Rashad was on his way to pick up Ferunell and he had room for one more. Rashad, Ferunell and I parked in front of Granny's house drinking a 40 oz.

After the night I had, I really needed this fellowship. We talked about everything from where we were to where we wanted to be. All three of us were in search of an exit out of the struggle. We wanted a better way and we were determined to make it happen. We decided to take an oath to carry to the grave, Loyalty Before Royalty. Nothing and no one would come in between our hearts.

My daddy called and we talked about our differences calling a truce right before graduation. I was ready to take that walk. On the day of graduation, all of us students were on one accord in our crimson caps and gowns. We walked into the arena to make history. After a few encouraging words, we began to receive our diplomas. As I walked across the stage, an entire section erupted into cheers and started throwing up the Tre. I saluted my people with my three fingers held high and made my stroll as the first in my immediate family to graduate and head to college. Oh, what a time to be alive. I wished Mama Bea and Stunna Bam were there to see this moment, but I could feel them walking with me. To close the ceremony, Shaquin and Keke started singing "End of the Road" by Boyz II Men bringing the whole class to tears.

For four years we walked the halls of Jack Yates together and we shared a lot of memories. We had become a family beyond blood and now it was time for us to go our separate ways to accomplish our goals and aspirations. Through all the good and bad times, we had each other, but now it was time for us to begin another chapter. I did not know where this road led, but I hoped to see more of the world and much better than what I knew. As we hugged each other and wiped our tears, we held something in our hearts that no one could take away. To the Jack Yates Class of 2010, I love you all, always and forever.

CHAPTER 8
THE STRUGGLE CONTINUES

In the months following graduation, I walked through the hood to capture a glimpse of what once was and what was still in existence. Some familiar faces had vanished into the wind, but their spirits still lingered. Some familiar faces reaped the benefits of "the family business" while taking cover from the hefty risks that accompanied their work. Some familiar faces still fell prey to drugs and begging for spare change to get their daily fix of bum's wine. *This cannot be all my people are worth. This cannot be what people see in me when I tell them I am from 3rd Ward.* I honestly grew tired of enduring and witnessing this struggle, but just like everyone else, I did not know how to escape it. A change of scenery seemed like the best bet at that point.

As I prepared for this transition, hanging out, talking and joking with friends seemed bittersweet. All I had ever known was 3rd Ward and what was inside the loop, and there I was preparing to leave it all behind. I was low-key scared, but I refused to show my fears to anyone. *What am I afraid of? This is something we always talked about growing up—leaving the hood one day to put our family on. I better suck it up and continue the grind and mission.* My daddy often told me stories of how he had received several great opportunities to leave the hood that could have been beneficial for him and the family, but he strayed away from each one. Now he was stuck in the hood and unsure of how to escape the curse. Many of his peers attested to how they and many of their classmates and friends were phenomenal athletes or were academically sound, but they allowed the inner-city blues to get the best of them and now they were stuck here telling tales of what they used to do, what they should have, would have and could have done if they had the opportunities that I now had. When I reflected on these stories, I thought of them as excuses and examples of what not to do.

I cannot come back home doing any of the things you can see walking down the street here. How can I be the change that everyone talks about but are afraid to be? How can I break this cycle and generational curse if I fall victim to my environment? Sometimes it sucks not having a good example of what to do, but I will take advantage of the examples of what not to do and make something out of it. That can be a gift and a curse because I know the law and what can happen by breaking the law, but that does not stop my palms from itching when I need and want something that I cannot afford. I wish my circumstances were different and I did not have to struggle with this demon on my shoulder that is telling me to go a different route than the one I am on. The only thing that is stopping me from making that choice is being fed up with the cards I was dealt and wanting to make a change and take the opportunities I was not born with.

My parents were not fortunate enough to have hell of money to buy me whatever I wanted when I wanted it. They were not able to pay for my college education or to buy me my first car. I noticed the pain in their eyes because they could not afford to do these things for us, so all I could think about at this point was not screwing this up. The last thing I wanted to do was loiter at a liquor store or corner store talking about what I used to do and the things I could have, should have and would have accomplished way back when. I decided to take this opportunity and run full speed ahead with it.

I hugged and kissed my mama and sister as I neared the security checkpoint of the airport. We all shed tears of joy and some of sadness because we had never been this far away from each other. My mama told me how proud of me she was as I picked up my bags and walked toward the checkpoint. My mind shifted to the business I had to take care of. *This trip is going to put us all on! I cannot mess this up.* I realized I was taking a big risk traveling to a place I had only been to once in my life. Not only because it was unfamiliar territory, but because I had made it through the checkpoint with bars and Vicodin in my pants and carry-on luggage. There I was talking about making a difference in my life yet bringing the ghetto right along with me.

I started feeling myself as the plane took off from Houston, taking me to my new home in Bethany, Oklahoma, a few miles away from Oklahoma City. *I hope this works out so I can come home with something no one in my family has.*

"Welcome to Oklahoma, Thadd!" My teammate greeted me as he helped me with my bags. A sense of excitement overwhelmed me along with a swarm of butterflies in my stomach. I was about to embark on my college football career while continuing my education. I was ready to get to work but still telling myself, *do not mess this up!* I hopped into the truck with my new teammate and left some of my worries behind at the airport.

Coaches and other teammates greeted me as we arrived at the welcome meeting. I felt accomplished just by being in the room. Equipment managers were lined up ready to fit us with our armor, which made me even more anxious. I still had a conditioning test to pass before I could really put in work. *I am about to take my game up another notch. I hope I am ready for this.*

On this new field, hours away from my hometown, I was determined to do work. The conditioning test began, and I found myself both pumped and anxious as hell. Whistles blew, bodies moved rapidly up and down the field, and people threw up their insides on the sidelines. It was intense. My time to ball out soon came, and there was no turning back at this point. I exhausted myself to show off the great shape I was in. No lie, I should have been working out and training more before I brought my ass out there. Just as I felt close to passing out on the field, I made it across the finish line. I passed the test, which prepared me to continue the mission. The coach debriefed then dismissed us until our early morning wake-up call. It was a job well done, but the grind had just begun.

Back in the dorm with my other roommates, we started getting acquainted with one another until we fell asleep. As usual, I could not sleep as I lied awake thinking about this new experience. This, too, is a gift and a curse because when I am in my head too much for too long, I begin to doubt certain choices and second-guess myself. I swear I hated ever having to experience people telling me what I could not and would not do out of hate. Being the scapegoat for other people's problems damaged me mentally and emotionally; I never really thought about it until that very night.

I wondered what was going on back at home. I felt alone even though there were two other people in the room. Because I still did not know them well, I wondered how we were going to mesh. I was black and from the hood and they were white and from the country. Not being racist, but I wondered if they would be cool with living with my ghetto ass for the duration of our stay. *How would they feel if they knew I came out here with drugs just in case I needed to make some moves? I am tripping. Let me go to sleep before wake-up call comes around.*

"Wake-up call, gentlemen . . . LET'S GO!" The coaches banged on our doors and set off the siren on their bullhorns to wake us all up.

Damn, I am tired as hell, but I must get to work for early morning workouts, meetings and practice. This is what I signed up for. No sleeping in on the job! We had to be at the field house by 5:30 a.m., so we all raced to make our way to our common destination. Speed and Strength at Yates used to be at 8 a.m. This was going to take some getting used to.

Strapping up my armor for the first time as a college athlete seemed bittersweet. I felt as if I was making history as I put on my helmet and pads. It was time to hit something.

"Let's see what that Texas football is like big H-Town!" A veteran player called me out.

Man, I must show him a thing or two now.

We stretched, huddled up to listen to the coach, and parted ways for individual position workouts. I felt pumped and nervous again as I waited for my turn in the drills. The horn blew and it was time for some real-live contact: Oklahoma drills! It was my time now. Though they slapped me with a red shirt at the last minute, I still vowed to put on for my family and hood.

Watching my teammates go at each other's heads fueled me as my turn approached. I dug in as I awaited the coach's whistle. Before I knew it, the guy in front of me and I fired out of our stance to make contact quickly. He tried to rip out of my block but could not, and my running back burst through his gap. I felt good about this practice and I grew eager to continue the good work.

With my first college football practice now over, I was hyped as I linked up with the other players from

Houston. I thought they would make this transition a bit easier, but I missed home already. *I'll just chill and get my mind right before we must hit up our evening workout.*

Something about the sound of a few forty-five plates clanking together makes a man feel like he is strong as hell. Heads bobbed left to right as a Lil' Boosie song played during our workout. Boosie's song "Bankroll" is the perfect hype song whenever it is time to hit the gym. Eating proved to be no problem at all in the weight room; it showed as I was able to lift with the upperclassmen.

I low-key did not think I belonged there. Though I appreciated the opportunity, I still was salty about not being at Oklahoma State. I believed I was D-1 worthy but settled for less by signing with a NAIA school. Not saying SNU is not a good school, but I believed I was better than what the university could offer. I used this as fuel to improve and to get to where I really wanted to be. Then again, I really missed being home. Leaving everything I had ever known was way harder than I expected. I had to fight through these thoughts and feelings before they overwhelmed me, but the struggle continued as I battled my mental demons. I remained in football to help tackle my issues, but it did not seem to be working as effectively as I had planned.

I had never been away from home for an extended period, so I soon found myself in a panic trying to find any little reason to leave and go back to 3rd Ward. One day I was in the shower when I saw the words, "Nigger go home!" carved into the wall. I perceived it as a sign and called my mama begging her to buy me a ticket to come back home. She managed to calm me down, helping me survive my first case of homesickness.

This did not negate the fact someone in the dorm did not like the idea of being surrounded by black teammates. With this and so many other realizations, I could feel myself losing sight of what I had set out to do in Oklahoma. I stopped attending practice and workouts and I lied in my depression all day while everyone was gone. Soon I became comfortable with being alone. I did not eat for a few days and barely took showers. I was down bad on myself and did not even know why. All I wanted to do was go back to the hood where I felt most comfortable. It was crazy because I was throwing away the opportunity to make something of myself. *What makes me any different than the people that sit on the corner all day back home? Why do I not give a damn about what happens to me from this point?* I eventually mustered up enough energy to get out of bed and get myself together. As I stood before the mirror, I stared deeply at myself. I was confused about the person I saw because it was not who I wanted to be. In that moment, I began to groom my thin beard and clean myself up. I was still unsure of who I was, but I became determined to figure things out.

I walked down to the lobby of my dorm building and people looked at me in the same disbelief I had minutes before.

"Damn, Thadd! I thought you went back home, bro."

I guess I was locked away in my room for much longer than I thought. To many, it appeared as if I had given up on the team, but I really gave up on myself. I was unsure of why I wanted to play football or even be miles away from all I had ever known. I was sure of one thing, though—I needed to make some money. I still had those pills I brought with me and I overheard some of my teammates talking about needing something. I had what they needed and they had what I needed, so I made it happen.

Over time I ran into some family from Tulsa who were in the game, too, and managed to get my hands on more things to distribute. I became more acquainted with my friends from Lawton and they had a taste for one thing—drank. Being from Houston, everyone from out of town automatically associated you with it and the funny thing about it, I could get it easily. I finally found an excuse to say to hell with football and instead focus on my education and getting money.

Some people questioned my decision to quit football, but I did not care one bit. They knew better than to try me because I was always ready to fight. My other boys from Houston and I were always in the lobby telling stories of how it goes down back home. Everyone was intrigued and wanted to hang out with us. To them it seemed as if we were from a foreign land.

Certain things about us only a few people could understand. My boy Big Ed understood me well. Ed had some concerns that kept him from football, so we hung out daily. We walked to an alley by the school every night to smoke and talk about life. We both aspired to make it out of the struggle and to become a great success. I often reflected on all those cold nights I had to endure back in the hood and how I never wanted to experience that again. I realized I had to get my shit together quickly or that would be my future.

While school appeared to be going well, money began to run low again. My aunt's friend sent me $200 a month, but it was not good enough for me. My palms started to itch again and my boy told me about some mean licks he had just hit. No lie, I wanted in, so I linked up with him on some moves. I always saw him riding in different cars with different girls, which let me know he had to be on his note with this grind.

One day I hitched a ride with him to talk business. So much for making a change for the better; I found myself doing things I said I would never do. At this point, I had to survive and make something shake. It was not like it was not a part of who I am. My family taught me better than this, but my environment presented options to satisfy my itch. *Do I care about being a part of the problem and a statistic? Hell no, I just want bread. I will worry about the consequences later. Whatever happens to me out here is just going to happen.*

Late night riding with my boy E and his girl through Oklahoma City became my new routine. Talking about money moves and smoking hell of Kush numbed all my worries. One night we made a stop at the store to re-up on cigars and soda for the drank we had just copped. As I exited the car, I saw E grab his girl's purse in search of something, but I asked no questions. I was on a mission, which was the only thing on my mind. We got our fixes and drove off to our spot. We talked about the next lick that E's girl and her friend were helping set up. It finally seemed as if things were falling into place.

We pulled up to the dorm and then we parted ways. I was high as hell, so I just wanted to take a shower and lie down for the night. I returned from my shower to see flashing lights on my wall and six missed calls from E. I called him back to hear bro tripping like some shit had just popped off. I started to think those flashing lights were for us.

"Bro stay in your room. The bitch called the laws on us and I am trying to get things straight."

I tried to figure out what E was talking about because we all were just riding and getting high together.

What would make this girl call the police on us? He eventually called back to tell me that the situation was handled and we were in the clear. Something still did not feel right, but I shrugged it off and made my way to bed.

One might ask, "How can you go from being hype about playing college football to selling dope and hitting licks?" When you are tired of your people telling you no every time you ask for things you need and want, you begin to take what you need and want. To many this might be senseless, but I would rather risk my life to survive. I was on the verge of returning to those cold nights with no lights again, so I made my move. It bothered me that all my friends in Oklahoma were fly, could buy the things they wanted when they wanted them, could go to parties, and were having the time of their life. I, on the other hand, was washing the same six shirts and few pants and shorts I had over and over just to have clean clothes.

I once overheard this girl tell her friend, "Damn, is that the only shirt he has to wear? He wore it like three times this week."

That really hurt my feelings and I felt ashamed. I hated seeing this struggle continue to run laps around me. Before anyone else could shame me, I decided to take matters into my own hands and take what the fuck I wanted.

It sucks that people will criticize you before they get to know you or even ask how they can help you. They would rather see you down so that they can point and laugh at you. I learned a long time ago that you would be fighting every day if you decided to fight the people that mock your struggles and transgressions. I decided to take on the struggle headfirst instead. Was I doing it the right way? No, I was not, but that is what came with the territory of being from the ghetto. You had to make a choice to either: do what you have to do and live or be conservative and do without.

I guess I will never shake the curses of being born into my family and being from 3rd Ward. It looks like what everyone said about me is true. Then again, I could be reassuring their opinions. I could be thinking too hard about everything that is going on. I tend to be deep in my head too much for too long, which causes many of my depressive and psychotic symptoms. I really need help, but I honestly cannot talk about this at all. Oh well, I will suck it up and continue with the move we have planned. I am still unsure about who I am and what I want to do, but I guess I will have to roll with the flow and see how this goes.

For anyone who sees this, I am sorry for being a statistic. I do not want you to judge me; just understand my blues so that you can help someone not make the mistakes I made.

CHAPTER 9
RISKING MY LIFE

One day, I rode through Bricktown with E, Shay and a couple of other guys. Shay was E's girlfriend and she had stumbled up on a jackpot for us this time. Shay was known for coming up off tricks and "ballers". She had recently met a truck driver who just so happened to move weight on his trips. Shay managed to get the alarm code, become friendly with the dog, and learn where he stashed his money and dope. Our plan was to run in, get the money and dope, and get out of there before anyone noticed anything. The guy was preparing to leave for a three-day trip to the Midwest, so the timing was perfect for us.

When the time arrived for things to go down, I had my gloves on and was ready for whatever. I felt those butterflies again, but I had to do what I had to do. Shay briefed everyone one last time on what was in the house and where to find it.

"Man look . . . y'all don't be on that extra shit when we get in here. In and out! Don't forget the mission." I had to make sure those guys had their minds right because they could not keep their sticky fingers under control. I just wanted the bread so that I could go home and enjoy fall break; I was beyond ready to kick it with my family and friends. I shook my thoughts away and decided to worry about fall break later. It was time to go to work.

Shay handled the door, alarm and dog before we hit the spot. After she said it was all clear, we were all up in this man's spot; there was no turning back. I focused on filling up my bag with bread while E looked for whatever dope buddy had in the house. E came up on a duffle bag with some ounces of powder and we began to make our way from the second floor. Those other fools tried to steal electronics, so we wasted time trying to get them and get out.

I heard a door slam and what sounded like a gun being chambered. *Man, we are stuck in a bad position because these dudes want to be greedy. It is enough in these bags to go around for all of us at least two to three times.* I then began to think about the risk approaching up the stairs. *Will we make it out alive or get jammed up? Hell, I do not know. All I know is we better figure it out or that is our ass. That is what I get for committing burglary of a habitation with some clowns.*

The footsteps inched closer and I signaled everyone else to stay back while I made whatever move I could. I observed the face of the silhouette on the wall as I swung a mean right jab. I was right about him having a gun because it fired off when he hit the wall due to the impact of the blow. He tumbled down the two flights of stairs and landed on the first floor knocked out cold. We had to burn out because we just knew someone had heard that gunshot. E tied the guy's hands behind his back and we dashed out of the house.

E stumbled and recovered his balance before hopping into the SUV. "Man, dog, shit that was crazy, bro!" E yelled all in my ear as Shay drove off to the spot.

I could not believe what had just happened in that house. Things quickly went south. Burglary of a habitation turned into a home invasion in what seemed liked seconds. Once we made it to OKC, I figured we were good. We split up the money and the other guys handled the work we found—a payday for a later day. Soon it was time to get high so that I could ease my mind and anxiety.

Back in the commons for dinner time, I was grateful that I was still here and we made it out of that house undetected. I ate with the crew and talked about our plans for fall break. They knew I would be in Houston, so some of them asked me for some oil. I could get it back with no problems for a quick little check. Some of my friends appeared to know what I did because they repeatedly told me to be careful.

I knew I needed to be cool, but it seemed as if the bread kept calling me. No matter how big or small, taking things that did not belong to me gave me a thrill. I thought back to that scene from *Menace II Society* when Caine's grandfather asked him if he cared whether he lived or died. In that moment, I felt like Caine because I honestly did not know. I had been in pain and enduring hell for a long time. If I had not knocked that dude out and he would have shot me, then that would have been my fate and there would have been nothing I could do about it. I knew that was a negative way to view things, but my ghetto had created this monster. Though I had walked out of that house alive and was about to visit home for the break, I just hoped none of my actions would come back to bite me in the ass.

As I sat in my window seat, I stared at the iconic skyline. I smiled from ear to ear as I jammed to Bun-B's verse of "Welcome 2 Houston". I was hyped about leaving and I had the same energy about coming home. It was such a great feeling that I wanted it to last forever. I had dreams of leaving the ghetto but in reality, the experience was not what I expected.

All I could think about was hugging and kissing my mama, sister and little brother as I walked to baggage claim. I saw them sitting from a distance, so I snuck up behind them to greet them. They were just as happy as I was, and I thought about how Faith had brought me back here. It was time to get a good home cooked meal and to figure out how to spend this bread.

It is crazy what one man can and will do for money. I risked my life to have security and material things I could not afford growing up. To be honest, I did not feel any more secure than I did before running up in that house. I thought spending money on Polo, Jordan and Nike would make me feel better but instead, I started looking over my shoulders even more. I expected Karma to run up on me with a pistol to my head to shake me down for everything I had and leave me for dead. I guess Faith kept her away from me this time. *How can I be the difference when I just added to the problem out here? This is how I know this is not for me and I need to get my act together before it is too late.*

A phone call from an OKC number interrupted my thoughts. "Hello, I am looking for Thaddeus Tolbert."

I confirmed my identity to the person on the other end of the phone.

"This is Detective Wilson with the Oklahoma City Police Department and I was wondering if you had time to come talk to me about a few things today."

My stomach dropped into my Polo boxers. I instantly thought about being in that house when I was supposed to be in class learning. I told him I was not in OKC now but would return after fall break.

"Make sure you come holler at me when you get back, man, so we can take care of this situation that your name came up in."

It all began to make sense now. I had called my boys earlier before going to the mall and they did not answer. E normally answered my calls, so I feared the worse. Karma was coming back for me and she was thirsty for blood. Because I could not enjoy being at the Gallo (the Galleria

Mall) anymore, I left to go cop a sack to blow. No matter how much weed I smoked, I could not shake this monkey off my back.

The time to return to school soon arrived, but I dreaded going back to face the piper. Despite the circumstances, I still had the oil my boy ordered and my palms itched for that bread. *How can I think about selling a pint at a time like this? What is this feeling that is coming over me? I am starting to not care about the consequences of my actions, and I booked a bus ticket to make sure I get this package back with no problems. My people are on my ass about not being back at school when I'm supposed to be, but I am not paying them any mind. This is my life and I do and move how I please.*

Still caught up in my thoughts, I hugged and kissed my family and departed on the eight-hour bus ride back to Oklahoma. *This might be the last time I get the chance to hug and kiss them in the free world. All I can do right now is text this girl from school. She says that she is digging me, but she has some baggage to clear up. Baby, I have a lot of baggage that comes along with me as well, so handle that and I will get with you when I get there.*

I woke up in OKC with a missed call and voicemail from one of my boys. I knew I had to hit him back ASAP.

"Bro, maaannn, that boy E on some other shit, bro!"

I could not help but think about the night he was spazzing out at the dorm. "Fam, what's poppin'?"

He told me E got caught up and his fingerprints came back on a gun at a house. I struggled to comprehend the situation. Only the owner of the house had a gun and no one touched it but him. I wondered how in the hell did E's prints come back on a gun found at the scene. Completely unaware of it at the time, E pulled out a tool on the owner, dropped it when he stumbled out of the house, and did not realize it nor tell anyone what happened. The story gets deeper from here, though. If you have not figured it out already, E started singing like a canary during his interrogation. To add insult to injury, he fit the description from other burglaries and he sang on the whole crew. Bro even told me E identified me as the ringleader of the licks. He did all of this before finding out they found his gun with his prints on it, after which his story changed quickly. Honestly, I thought about smoking E in that moment but figured that would make me look even guiltier. Besides, I had never killed anyone though the thought often crossed my mind. My mind cleared as a pretty lady greeted me with a big smile, hug and kiss on the cheek, but I had some business to handle before I made my move on her.

My friend dropped me off at the dorm and took my bags to another location because I could not get caught up with this oil me. I swiped my card to get into the dorm, but it did not work. The residential officials had turned my card off, leaving me in an even tighter jam.

"Mr. Tolbert, glad you are back, but we still have to talk." Detective Wilson had found me, so it was time to face the piper.

I left with him on my own accord because I was ready to get it over with. We arrived at the station and my heart raced 100 mph. I should have thought about all the consequences before running up in that house, but the damage had already been done.

Sitting at a table in an interrogation room for what seemed like an eternity, I recalled seeing a similar room on The First 48. Some people folded up and started crying; some people gave off a guilty vibe; some remained G and stiff up in there. I aimed to do the latter.

142

Detective Wilson walked in and began the interrogation. "I see you are from H-Town. What brings you to OKC?"

I explained how I was attending school and tried to play football, but it did not work out.

"So, what do you do now that you do not play football anymore?"

The honest answer: "I rob, run in houses, and sell drugs, sir." I could not cop out on myself or anyone else, so I stuck to the being a schoolboy and poet front. While I was not lying, I still could not tell him the whole truth.

"So, how do you know Mr. Harold?"

"That's my boy from school and he is down with my people from Tulsa." I honestly hated him for me putting me in this position, but no one told me to agree to it anyway. Everyone knew the code of the street though: I did not hear anything, see anything or say anything. Before

I knew it, Wilson told me I was free to go and walked me out of the station.

On the way back to school, he gave me some good game that I will carry with me forever. "Do not give a man the opportunity to play God in your life. Handle your business and be the difference that you want to be."

To my young brothers or sisters reading this book, take heed to my lessons and watch the footsteps you follow. You do not want to step in the same shit I got on my soles. Do not be too proud to learn or listen to someone who wants the best for you and have been where you are. The game is changing only because the players before you did not *show* you the right way. To the OGs and elders, be a better example and cut out that "do as I say" attitude. While we can learn something from each other, you cannot expect the up and coming generation to listen and understand if you do not take the time to do the same.

I risked my life to learn this lesson, so please do not let my words be in vain.

CHAPTER 10
BACK TRIPPIN'

After a while I found myself back in my comfort zone—3rd Ward Houston, TX. Things did not go according to plan in Oklahoma and I had to go home to get my mind and shit together. Sadly, I had to leave my girl behind but like my daddy always told me, "I have never seen a man lose women chasing money, but I have seen a man lose money chasing women."

I had a long list of things to do before applying to Prairie View A&M University and even more to get straight. I worked at Target to make legit money while I prepared to knock out classes at Houston Community College. I had never taken the legit route before, so I gave it my best. However, I still had an itch for more money. I guess I had not learned my lesson from the break I received in OKC. I was glad I was able to escape from the craziness up there, but I had to resist the temptation of the street life in my ghetto. I did not know how much longer I could take of standing on my feet all day, so I decided to get with some of the bros to see what I could get my hands on.

Whether you went to Dodge City, The Bottom or The Bricks, you could get your hands on whatever you wanted for the right ticket. It did not matter if you were a consumer or distributor—it was all good in my ghetto. It seemed like selling white or hard was the way to make good money, but my boy Wayne refused to put me on because he thought I did not belong in the streets. I could not do anything but respect what he said because it was the truth. I managed to beat charges that many of my peers had served time for. I knew the risks that came with being in that life, but I had already convinced myself that jail or death was better than being without.

My mama worked two jobs just to get by and my daddy lectured me about not being in school. If I sat there and waited for someone to hand me something, then I would be doing myself a great injustice. I just did not want to get caught in someone else's house again. Yes, I made it out intact, but I could not promise I would not do it again. *I guess I should keep working this job until it is time for me to move around. Maybe I will get blessed with the opportunity of getting my hands on something. To hell with this—I am going to shoot the dice on this and pray I hit.*

It seemed as if I made my move right on time. I had to get a series of dental work done and they prescribed me

Vicodin. I immediately knew I was going to sell them to someone who really needed them. My little bro had already told me how the white kids at his school would be clucking for pills and were willing to pay three times the rate in the hood. I showed my little bro love for pointing me in the right direction.

My school refund was due to hit soon, so I knew I would be good for a while. I even had enough to pay for my trip to see my fam in Tulsa, OK. Yeah, I know I was tripping for returning to Oklahoma after escaping a jail sentence, but I could not pass up this opportunity. Fam said he had a few plays set up that could get me enough bread to take care of myself for a while when I get to PV. How could I say no to making money? Whatever it took to make it happen. I know I am now conflicting myself because I said I would not do certain things, but he could get his hands on some good work. If you do not know what this is, do yourself a favor and stay in the green zone. If you do know, then you know where I am going with this. You also know the risks that come with holding weight like that. If I knew then what I know now, I would have kept my ass in Houston, but I hopped on that bus for what seemed like easy money.

I missed seeing my fam in Oklahoma and they could not believe I had made it back. My dawg T was like a cousin to me. We fought for each other, stole for each other and if it came down to it, we would squeeze the trigger for one another. When he called me for the plays, I planned to come by any means. We both had dreams of leaving the hood for better opportunities even though we planned to push something into the community that had been more harmful than helpful to most. I guess our own basic needs come before anyone else's when it comes to survival. That was not on my mind, though; I just wanted us to make it out of this shit intact so that we could live it up when we became successful the legal way. Until then, we had work to do before we could return to the H.

I stood at attention with a few other guys while T made the transactions with a dealer. I was on edge but sort of relieved because this was our final stop before heading to the H. Making 5k in a couple days was cool with me because I had never seen that much money up close and I really did not have to do much. After completing the transaction, we bailed out to the spot to split the bread before going our separate ways.

T and I rode to his mama's house to gather the rest of our things so that we could hit the road. J-Dawg's "Back Trippin'" started playing and it seemed as if he had been watching us because he surely told our story.

"Man . . . about time we get the fuck up out the hood for a little bit. What's good on that PV move, B?"

T knew how serious I was about hopping on the football team when I got to PV. Hell, he wanted to go to college himself because he knew he could not keep living this way.

As we continued to drive, I really tuned into J-Dawg's lyrics. "I'm getting my Menace II Society on. Act like Caine cousin and get your whole face blown." You must see the movie to understand the true meaning behind those words.

Though the mission was complete, I still had a bad feeling because I knew I did not belong in the game. We could not take any of it back, though; we could only move forward.

T and I made sure that we had everything we needed before we hit the road for Prairie View. Mama wanted us to eat a good meal before we left but we had forgotten a few things, so we headed to the local corner store. It felt like the walk I took through 3rd Ward before I left for football camp. Now I was about to introduce my boy to college life.

Seeing some familiar faces and hearing some encouraging words made me feel as if this was going to be a great opportunity for T and I. We purchased a beer to split on the walk back from the store. Back in the Tre, T and I used to share a single cigarette while we walked and talked about life. Years later, we were still kicking it and making plans.

The voice of a familiar friend interrupted our conversation. "Aye, Thadd . . . T-Wash! What it is my dawgs?"

We threw up our arms in excitement yelling up to our boy as he stood on the balcony of this duplex. We posted up and finished the beer while we waited for our boy to come down. A split second later, glass shattered from doors flying open and the streets were filled with screams and gunfire. T and I fell right into a trap and now our plans were no longer certain.

If I do not make it out of this alive, tell my people I love them. I am sorry for jumping off that porch. I am sorry for not living up to the potential that is embedded in me, but I was foolish enough to fall victim to senselessness. Daddy, I know you did not plan on this for your son, but this is what happens when you think you know it all and do not give a damn about consequences. I have always wondered if my funeral would be packed. It looks like my family is about to find out the hard way. Could there still be hope for us? Hell, I sure hope so. Faith, if you can hear me, we are in some deep shit again and need you more than ever.

As we ran for our lives down an alley, another door flew open with more gunfire. I felt my entire left side drop to the ground as I ran, but I managed to regain my balance and run harder. I had been shot in the arm and all I could think about was getting to T's house. He quickly cut the other way because he was faster than me and the shots continued to increase. Once I spotted him, I slightly picked up my speed to catch up.

Stepping out of the alley to run across the street, I spotted T already in the middle of the street. I then heard a loud boom and T dropped right where he stood. I could not believe my eyes. Fam's white shirt turned red almost instantly. The gunshots dissipated and police sirens replaced the screams. I ran to pick up T, but he was in bad shape. His pupils were beyond dilated, and he was gasping for air to talk. All I could see was the house across the street and I captured that image in my mind. We had almost made it. We were that close and fell short.

I am really in my dawg's blood trying to comfort him until help gets here.

T caught his breath enough to say, "Damn, fam . . . we almost made it. I'm sorry I can't go with you this time.

We should have never done this shit. Finish strong and never . . . look . . . back."

As the cops pulled up and ran to our aid, T trembled and died in my arms. Before we got the chance to leave and put our plans into play, my fam took his last breath as I held on to him tightly.

I could feel a piece of me leaving right along with him. You would think we were on the set of a movie and the director was about to yell cut to break from this intense scene. However, the scene before me was not from a television show or movie. There was no script or any chances to redo a take. Once you made a mistake in this reality, you could not take it back or act like you did not do it. What is done, is done. We came close to leaving all this bullshit behind us, but Faith's evil sister Karma came to collect her debt. T's life was the cost and now I was stuck with the vision of seeing my boy die in my arms covered in our blood.

The officer helped me up after I closed T's eyes and kissed his forehead. I was so numb that I forgot I was shot as well. It was not a big deal to me because I was still here. I honestly wished it was me in T's place or that it could have been me lying next to him under a sheet. On the inside, I still cried out for help even though the EMTs and the police were on the scene. I could still hear the gunshots. I could still hear the screams and glass shattering. I could still hear T's voice. I could still see his smile. I could still feel his body in my arms. *We almost made it to our destination, but now I am left here to travel this road alone, Faith. I cannot believe you left me hanging again. Now what am I going to do?*

I walked into T's funeral dressed up in all black inside and out. It had been two weeks, but I still felt numb. My shoulder hurt like hell and I fought through it the best way I could. I had lost my best friend over a few funky ass dollars. Five thousand dollars was not worth T's life at all. It was going right into the ground with him because the fam did not have life insurance. In reality, it seemed as if we made those moves just to cover his funeral arrangements. *We damn sure did not see it this way before hand, but this is what is it now. Is it selfish of me to wish it was my folks burying me on top of Mama Bea instead?*

Walking behind the reverend with T's mama holding my right arm and T's stepdad's left arm, the reality set in that my dawg was really lying there in a casket in front of everyone. I could feel his mama getting weak and I did my best to hold her up as we walked up to the casket. She kissed his cheek and rubbed his chest as she whispered, "I love you, Mama's baby," then walked to her seat with her husband.

I could not believe my eyes. *This was not part of the plan! I guess it is true what they say, when you say this is your last lick, it really is your last in some form or fashion. People say I am blessed to be here to tell this story, but sometimes I feel cursed because I can still feel this pain. I can still feel T dying in my arms in the middle of the street. This cannot be the way at all. I really have to get my shit together. See you on the other side my good friend.*

Taking that last ride with T to his final resting place left me feeling confused. We should have been in the H getting ready to go to PV and making plans to grow older together. Instead, we were putting his shell in the ground. No one should feel this pain, but this is the price you pay when you want to be a street nigga. Truthfully, I am far from a street nigga; that is not who I was raised to be. This was a choice I made to fit in and belong. I grew tired of people laughing at me over things I could not afford, and I made a dumb decision. I was no better than the ones who made this decision before me.

I must make this trip without my boy next to me, but he is forever in my heart. His last words are etched in my mind so that when I tell my story, I am telling his.

T, I love and miss you every day. If I could take a trip down memory lane, I would tell you that I love you and how bad of an idea it was to do what we did. Though it was all a misunderstanding, it cost you your life and changed ours forever. I got us no matter what. I will make the best of this opportunity that I almost squandered. I promise to make you proud and do something big not only for us, but for the world. I will tell that young man that has the feelings we had how much material things and fame are not worth their life. I will tell that young lady how precious she is to the world and how a man should not define who she is. You have taught me a lot out here and it is time for me to carry on. It is an honor to be your relative through loyalty and Christ. Many may never understand what that means.

CHAPTER 11
ABOUT MY BROTHERS BUSINESS

Here I am . . . at home dealing with these demons and intrusive thoughts. All I hear are gunshots and cries around me. I keep thinking about T and how my boy went out over some B.S. I wish I was not here to deal with this pain, but this is my reality and I must deal with it before it takes over me entirely. I have come too far to just lie down and be defeated like this. I have a plan and it is time to execute it. My daddy is on my ass about wanting to go to PV, but this is my life; I must do this! If I live life based on what people want of me, I will easily perish from a life that I did not ask for nor want.

My brothers and I have been talking about our plans of making it out

the hood and being able to provide for our family. There is a lot of

work to be done and it will happen by any means.

My fresh start at Prairie View neared and I tried to prepare my mind and body for this transition. My shoulder injury prevented me from putting in any work for football, but I believed I was strong enough to get active again. I wanted to be ready for whenever I received the opportunity to be on the team, so I would do whatever it took to get back into the swing of things.

Everyone in 3rd Ward had been grinding since the beginning of the summer. The streets were hot and busy, so I tried to stay clear. I watched over my shoulders almost every other step. I knew this was no way to live, but my choices and environment had left a scar on my mind that might never heal. Bodies still dropped and the heat intensified all around me. I needed a release and I honestly could not wait to go to PV. It would be a while before I returned, which was all with good interest and my sanity in mind. In the meantime, I needed to put in some good work and I knew the perfect person to help me.

God please protect my family and friends from ever having to feel this feeling that I am feeling. I bottle up my pain and walk around with a facial display of it on the daily. I know everything you do has a reason for it that we will not understand, but I pray for understanding, knowledge and vision to see the footsteps that are pressed in the sand for my guidance. I am beyond lost right now and I want to find my way out of these mental and physical traps. I understand this is what you have written for me well before my earthly existence, so questioning will not change the outcome. I just ask that you may please, please, please heal my ghetto.

Even though I prayed, I still struggled to understand life was not about when I wanted things to happen and how I expected them to happen. This battle belongs to the Heavenly Father and whenever He is ready for you, He will come for you. You must have your affairs together because that moment could happen at any time. That might explain why I felt as if I had yet to accomplish anything and death seemed to inch closer to me.

Just when I thought shit could not get any worse, it did. Trouble and confusion surrounded me. My heart grew heavy and my body froze. I closed my eyes and opened them after a moment of meditation just to realize I was not stuck in a bad dream. I became paralyzed from the thought of carrying out this mission with one less comrade. *How can society expect us to thrive in these circumstances?*

After composing myself, I expected to wake up to a productive day, but simply logging onto Facebook shattered my expectations: "R.I.P. Rashad Lionhearted Minix. A true Lion forever."

It seemed like no matter how much I worked my ass off to prosper and make progress, I constantly lost the things and people I loved dearly. I acted as if nothing was wrong, though, and carried on with the rest of my day. However, I constantly saw Rashad's face or heard someone talking about memories of him from high school. I could even hear his voice and laugh as I reflected on our own memories, but I refused to believe my brother was gone. We had so many goals to accomplish. *How can he up and leave me like this? No, he is not gone; someone is playing a sick joke on us. This cannot be real. This cannot be life! Damn, why does this hurt so bad, but I feel so numb?*

As the day progressed, I learned more details about what had occurred earlier that morning. It troubled me that my bro Ferunell was involved in the shooting with Rashad, but it relieved me to know he had survived and was expected to make a strong recovery. I just could not understand it. How could someone resort to that sort of violence with souls like Rashad and Ferunell? We fought like all brothers do, but things never got that serious. I knew there was more than one side to this story and I hoped to hear the person responsible for this tragedy speak his peace.

A troubling day of overthinking and disbelief turned into a night of reflecting and weed smoking. I had lost several people in my life—T's death was still a fresh wound that I struggled to accept—but this one was a nightmare. *He cannot be gone . . . this was not supposed to happen this way.* My thoughts raced constantly as I felt a cool breeze blow in my direction. I exhaled the Kush smoke, took a deep breath and broke down in tears. *This dude really took my brother away from us and this shit is not fair. We have barely been out of high school one year and been in college just as long. We are nowhere near where we wanted to be and had great plans of going a great distance in* life. I guess we will never know what we could have accomplished together.

Just the thought of my bro having a little one on the way triggered the tears even more. Another breeze brushed across my face and my tears followed. I quickly gathered myself before going back into the house; I could not let anyone see the full extent of my hurt and pain.

Faith, Faith, Faith, you are making it hard for me to believe in anything anymore. I do my best to be righteous, pray, and do the right thing, but look at what I am getting in return. I feel like I am playing this game of life with a bad hand. I know that everything is for a reason that I may never understand. I want you to know that I will never give up or in. You can take everything and everyone that I love, but I will still stand tall until you take me out of my misery. This life I live is hell, but just as in my favorite poem, "my head is bloody, but unbowed." My brother's vessel may be empty, but his spirit is within me. For as long as I live, the world will know of the great man that has helped me persevere through his eagerness to uplift.

Another loved one gone, another funeral to attend, another scar to add to the growing collection in my mind. I began to wonder when these senseless killings would end. Then again, it seemed like the norm because it was one of the only times a large group of us gathered together.

I know I am tired of being in front of a casket, but we are all destined to be there one day, right? I often picture myself lying in a casket in front of my family. I feel like that should have been me not too long ago. My mama, daddy, brothers and sisters walking up to say their last goodbye with tears in their eyes. The funeral director walks up and closes the lid on me then I wake up. My bros are outside blowing the horn for me to come out. Let me get out of here so we can go pay our respects.

Seeing a black hearse parked in front of a church really does something to you. Your heart rate increases, your breaths get shorter and your stomach slowly fills with butterflies. You begin to ponder how you will remember your loved one and how you would have never imagined having to say goodbye. These thoughts danced around my mind as we gathered ourselves to walk inside.

Damn . . . my bro is really lying there peacefully. He felt a lot of pain while taking his last breath, but he asked God to be with him before leaving this wretched place. I touched his chest and began to cry because I knew I could never feel his bear hugs, kisses on the cheek, or sneak attacks as he jumped on my back. I only had the distant yet close memory of his laughs that got us kicked out of class, the long talks we had as we rode through the hood and the plans we had of making it out.

I touched my chest to feel my heartbeat and whispered, "Loyalty Before Royalty." We vowed to take this oath to our graves. Bro was a man of his word because he did just that—a true reflection of character you cannot question and one I miss dearly.

As I glanced around the packed church, I could see Rashad had touched a lot of people. I had never seen a funeral with an overflow section. It amazed me to see how one man could influence the lives of so many people from so many different roads in life. It was an honor to have Rashad as a friend and as a brother. *Farewell my brother; I will see you when that time comes.*

In the weeks following Rashad's funeral, I realized it was time to continue the mission. Ferunell appeared to be recovering physically, but I could tell the shooting was taking a toll on his mind. I can recall hearing Cal Wayne's "About My Brother's Business" playing in the background thinking I had to make this second chance count so that I could free my family from these unfortunate circumstances and break this curse. I hated feeling like I was not worthy or walking around with juju on me. I constantly told myself: *I just have to make it. Seems like all the people who have ever believed in me are dead now, so I must be my own motivation. This work is not going to do itself and excuses do not pay the bills. I am going to do big things at PV and will show the world what it means to be Lionhearted and 3rd Ward to the heart.*

I left 3rd Ward behind again to make an impression in Prairie View, TX. I did it for all the ones that could not make it, but this move was especially for me. Because I was behind schedule, I had to work my ass off to get back on track. No distractions, drama, B.S., trouble or heat from the streets—or so I thought. I had a new lady from Cali in my life and she seemed to be down for me. I was excited to see how this fresh start would play out.

I sure do hope and pray that I can make big things happen here. I refuse to go back to the hood empty-handed. That is not part of our plans and I will not make it an addition to the pages we have yet to fill. Business will go on as usual.

CHAPTER 12
REINCARNATED

A breath of fresh air is exactly what I needed. It finally seemed as if everything was coming together like I had planned. I stumbled across some familiar faces at PV, so home was well within reach. Even the people I barely knew were warm and accepting. I hoped I could maintain this momentum without losing focus again. However, the thoughts and dreams I had from day to day still affected my ability to focus at times.

One night I dreamt I was back at Yates in the cafeteria with my boys. We were having a good time, laughing and cracking jokes as usual. As I opened the door to walk outside, I looked up and saw Rashad. It captured us both by surprise. He ran into my arms and gave me a big hug and a kiss on the cheek.

He told me, "Thaddo, bro, I really love and miss you, man. I know life is not the same and will never be the same, bro. You must carry on with the work but know I will always be right here with you, bro. Always remember me and watch after my family. Please, brother, watch after my little girl and teach her about her daddy, bro. I love you and never forget that. Loyalty before royalty, my brother."

I woke up with tears pouring down my cheeks and a warmness near my heart. I could feel where his spirit had touched me. In that moment I realized this was much bigger than me and I had no choice but to make this happen. I would be carrying on a legacy while building one of my own. The impact my brother made on my life would not be forgotten and his mother, father and daughter would know who he was and still is to me. We took an oath years ago and though he is not physically here with me, those words are forever bonded.

I adjusted to school well, grinding to finish what I had started. Before I could get comfortable, more trouble surfaced in my life. The woman I had been giving my all to had been sleeping around on me during my trips back home. I once overheard a suspicious conversation between her and her cousin and some of my boys had seen her being mischievous as well. Her deception truly cut me to the core. *I am trying to fight these demons to make a difference in my life, but it seems like I just cannot get a break. Tomorrow is my birthday, but right now I just want to end it all right here right now.*

It might sound silly that I wanted to end my life over a woman, but my woes ran much deeper than that. Have you ever grown tired of struggling to make it through the struggle? I grew tired of getting the short end of the stick. Every time I thought I had a great momentum, something jumped up and grabbed my leg to slow me down. *No matter how hard I fight to keep the wheels rolling, I am sinking further and further into the mud. I am struggling for air right now and I just want to be away from this misery and wickedness. They say you can go to hell for doing what I want to do, but it honestly cannot be as bad as the hell I have been living. I cannot do living anymore; I must end this once and for all.*

As I walked to the kitchen to grab a knife, a sudden knock at my door and a sweet voice stopped me in my tracks. I walked over to the door and looked through the peephole to see it was my good friend Desiree coming over to hang out. I opened the door and she greeted me with a big hug. She had no idea how much I really needed that hug. She sat down on the couch to roll up a joint to bring in my birthday with me. I stood there thinking, *Damn . . .*

God really works in mysterious ways. I was so close to cutting myself and watching my misery, hurt, anguish, pain, disappointment, anxiety, trauma, frustration, promises and whole life pour out of me. This is not my first nor last time contemplating suicide and having a plan of how to do so. Lord, I really need you and I need you now.

Even though an abundance of birthday love surrounded me, I still felt so alone. I did not understand what this girl had triggered deep inside of me and I hated this feeling. I faked my smile when people walked up to me with warm greetings. One group of familiar friends was able to see past my fake smile and gave me long, sincere hugs. Those hugs allowed everything I had bottled up to escape through the tears that poured down my cheeks once again. Real love will do it every time. You never know what people are going through and how much hope you can give someone with just a simple hug or conversation. The night before I wanted to end my life, but now I saw a new life ahead of me. I should not have allowed anyone to have this much power over me. I wondered what the collateral damage would have been had Desiree not knocked on my door. In the midst of my thoughts, I realized I meant something to other people, which helped me understand my significance in this world. A cease to my existence before my time would have caused even more pain than I ever could have imagined. With all the losses and anguish I had experienced, why in the hell would I want to pass that on to anyone else?

I realized I had put a strain on myself for many years because I talked about believing but had not walked the walk of Faith. I lacked not only Faith in myself but also unconditional Faith in God. Because I am made in His image, not believing in myself made it hard for me to believe in Him.

With just a little belief, you can see the light within the darkness if you lean on your Faith and not completely on your sight. There is always much more than meets the eye and it took years of going through hell and making mistakes to see beyond the things I had seen. On September 14, 2011, I kneeled in submission to the God in me and fasted from all distractions so that I could take on my new form. The epiphany of my reincarnation was alive and well.

My mind is in a right space, my head is held high, and my feet are planted firmly into the ground. I am content with the man I see in the mirror today, but I do not see myself being in this position tomorrow. Time is passing by faster and faster, so you must keep your feet moving or it will pass you right by. Friends and family will become memories, the home front will have new features, and even more would have, could have, should have stories will be written. William Ernest Henley ended the poem Invictus by stating, "I am the master of my fate: I am the captain of my soul." I have great control over my life and the direction in which I walk. We all have a choice and we need to realize it while we still have a say in what we can do. The dynamics change when you get that inmate number or are being lowered into the ground. I have seen both happen way too many times in my lifetime and I want to stray away from those things.

I made the move to Prairie View to model perseverance. I wanted the children, my peers and my elders to read a positive story about that little, dirty fat kid from the ghetto that made it and gave his community something to hope and aspire for. We did not need any more news stories about how I was another statistic, menace to society, habitual offender, body count, or reason why uppity white people and politicians think I am the reason why my people deserve to be caged like animals.

If you write your own story and live it through, you do not have to worry about anyone's lies or perception being added into your mix. Even if the media presents a negative image of you, character and credibility will take you far. I used to care what people thought about me, but it does not even matter to me now because my character and loyalty project louder than my voice. Now that I know what I know now, I can turn that struggle into fuel for my engine and I am running until my tank is on "E".

Cal Wayne said you have to take me as I am. When a big dog barks, you better listen; when a lion roars, you better be attentive; and when the teacher is at the board, you better take notes. If you fail to listen, pay attention or take notes, then you will miss all the details you need to sharpen your iron. If you do not have a sharp mind, then you do not have the capabilities to sharpen your brothers' iron. Miseducation had been a great injustice for my community well before the first black family on the block made that move from Louisiana in 1947 in pursuit of better opportunities. They may have not accomplished what they wanted to, but the birth and life of their grandson will be a great addition to their legacy.

As I collect dean's list and honor roll awards, I realize I am breaking the family curse. Everyone is capable of being more than they are today, but most of them do not listen to the big dog, lion or teacher. They take the road most traveled by the would have, could have, should have clan. I am content with the route that I am traveling today, but I do not see myself standing in the same spot tomorrow. I need more to take this walk with me, but they must make sure they do not walk in the shit that I have stepped in.

CHAPTER 13
PERSEVERANCE/BE HUMBLE

Years ago, many people told me I would never make it out the hood and I would be like the ones that came before me. They wrote me off well before I received the opportunity to tell my story. Against all odds, I prepared to make history on The Hill as senior year approached. To be the first in my family to earn a degree was a big deal . . . a *very* big deal. You hardly ever saw any stories like mine being told on television. There was once a time I knew about college only because my daddy expressed the importance of going and I watched college sports on television. A few teachers may have mentioned it also, but how could I think of college as a possibility with my mind constantly in survival mode? I just focused on being alert for that next ass whipping. *I do not think I have to worry about those anymore. Well, at least I do not think that I do.*

Football may not have worked out, but I am thankful that I still have my education. I miss the game dearly and would do anything to be on the field still, but God may have other and better plans for me. Classes are going well, so we will see how things play out. My boy YaYa and I are in class every day talking about the next moves and I can honestly say that things are looking very promising. If I follow this plan and stay clear of negativity, I will be able to walk across that stage in May with no problems. Absolutely nothing can stop me with this momentum that I have built up.

Staring at the world through the rear-view mirror of my red Charger, I could see the past becoming a distant memory. I was feeling good and looking good, thinking this must have been how Cain felt riding in that 5.0 on Ds. However, riding in style came with a price. I could feel eyes on me as I reversed into my parking spot, so I routinely put my gun on my hip as I exited the whip and walked to my room. I knew I was supposed to be making a change for the better, but I was still shell shocked from my environment. I would rather get caught with it than without it. The boys on the first floor received a lot of traffic, so I could not be too careful. If you know what I mean, then you know and feel me.

Working two part-time jobs and being a full-time student proved to be difficult at times. I had responsibilities and no one was going to hand me a damn thing. With so many titles to juggle, I had to be disciplined, vigilant and attentive to details. One false move and one slipup could have cost me everything I had worked hard for or even my life. At such a young age, I had already witnessed these things in my life. I would be turning twenty-two years old that weekend, four years past the year people told me I would not live to see. *Here's to major accomplishments coming out the ghetto and to adding to the statistics in a good manner.*

That year I celebrated a milestone in a major way with great people surrounding me. I really wanted to visit the gun range with a special lady, but those plans changed. Everyone still enjoyed themselves, so I did not mind the change of plans. After the night ended back at my room, it was time to unwind and prepare to get back to work.

Midterms inched closer, meaning I needed to be prepared to kill my exams. This was not a game, drill or play. Every day and night, I fantasized about hearing my name being called at graduation. The Baby Dome would ignite with cheers as my people screamed my name at the top of their lungs. *It feels good to be celebrated while you are still here to enjoy the festivities. I wish my peers who are no longer here could experience this moment. I still have a few months to go, but it pays to be optimistic.*

The reality that I was running late for a midterm review soon crushed this fantasy. I found myself all over the place scrambling to get ready and sprint to class, which was not geographically far away but still a great distance in my head. I left my car in "Phase 3" across campus, so driving was out of the question. I ran my ass off to get to class on time and made it just as the professor walked in. After my small victory, I figured it might be a good day after all. Class ended just as quickly as it started, so I hurried to get my car and headed to the breakfast stop in Hempstead. You know a brother had to get his eat on.

Feeling full and weighed down from a big breakfast plate, I could really use a nap. I was in the car with a group of friends in route to campus when I missed a call from the phases. I had been waiting for a package, so I called back thinking I had something to pick up at the clubhouse.

I gave the caller my name and she replied, "May you please confirm your room number?"

After I recited the number, she dropped an unexpected package on me. My heart sank to my stomach as she stated, "We did an administrative room check and found a loaded pistol in a nightstand drawer. There is a zero-tolerance policy on weapons in our dorms, so you will be evicted. Your weapon has been confiscated by the police and you have to report to them for more details."

Damn, I really messed up this time, huh? Out here moving like I am still in the hood and made a careless move; a move that can cost me everything. How can I let everyone down like this? How can I go back to the hood and have everyone tell me how they told me so? How can I tell my parents that I really fucked up this time? How can I get the chance to hear my name being called now? My mind is going through a frantic rush right now, but I just need to be cool, own up to this mistake, and learn from it. Everything is going to be alright . . . right?

No everything was not alright. I had to vacate the premises immediately, the police took my "mugshot" for the no trespass ban they placed on me for all the campus dorms, and Chief Stephens chewed me the hell up. Chief Stephens was in command of the university police and we had established a great rapport being that she knew I was aspiring to pursue the military and law enforcement. It required great discipline to be involved with both law enforcement and the military and she did not hesitate to confront me about my poor decision making. I knew it was careless and I had to face the music, even if the sound became deafening.

I struggled to find a last-minute residence because I could not return home with this fuck up starring me down. I could hear my daddy's voice already—the last thing I needed to hear. I needed to fix my mistake on my own without all the negativity. Eventually, my boys Devin and Coby allowed me to crash with them as I awaited my fate with student conduct. It seemed as if I was on trial fighting for my life waiting on the jury to return with the verdict. All I could think about was how one mistake that did not cause any bodily harm could possibly cost me all my hard work and my future career. However, I understood the situation could have been unfavorable for the person who found the gun and the university had to consider the safety of thousands of people. *Whatever happens, happens and I must accept my consequences as a man. I just know that THIS will not stop me from my dreams and aspirations.*

The verdict was in . . . I had been suspended for the fall semester and would be placed on conduct probation upon my readmission. Honestly, I could live with the decision and I was thankful I had time to get myself together and handle my business. Just as I began to regain my momentum, life slapped me with yet another mishap.

The landlord is kicking us out and I am stuck with finding a new place to lay my head. I do not know what it is, but I am too proud to go back home for some reason. I strongly feel like this is something that God hit me with to handle on my own accord. There is only one problem: this pride will be forcing me to sleep in my car tonight. Lord, if you can hear me, please send help right now.

"What's up, Thaddo, you good?" My boy Donovan hit me up and I could not be any happier than I was in that moment. He continued, "I was just checking on you and seeing how you are holding up. Where you at now?"

It seemed as if God hit me in the gut and made me swallow my pride because I confessed to Donovan I was living in my car and did not know where I was going to sleep that night. Without hesitation he invited me over to crash at his spot. You really do see who is down for you when you are down bad on your ass. I happily accepted the invitation and hurried over to his crib. He greeted me at the door with a dap, a hug and a drink—I needed all three.

Donovan and I sat down and we began to talk. "Man, you know you are my dog and more than welcome to crash when you need. My girl is picking up some food and stuff now, so we got you tonight."

My daddy always told me a nigga will get you drunk before he will make sure you are fed and have a bed. I was glad Donovan did not fit that description. Because of his generosity, I could eat, shower, sleep and get my mind ready to grind the next day. I thank God every day for people like Devin, Coby and Donovan. I did not mind sleeping in my car ducked off somewhere, but they all extended their love to me when I needed it the most. I will never forget that for as long as I shall live.

With Faith, determination, hard work and a great support system, I survived my sanction and soon found myself back at work on The Hill. I had a new sense of mind and became even hungrier to reach graduation. Even though I had to take seven classes to graduate, my hunger fueled me to take on anything that stood in my way—even if it was the woman I thought I would spend the rest of my life with. To see how much I had grown and how much I had outgrown certain situations truly opened my eyes. I felt as if it needed to happen. If I was going to make it far, then I had to shed off the dead weight. Do not get me wrong:

once I love someone, that love lasts forever, but that does not mean I have to include that person in my plans once I have outgrown them. I wish them the best and want them to know they will always have a place in my heart regardless of where life takes us.

As I approached the final countdown to graduation, I thanked God for every lesson and blessing. We have always measured the game by who is the winner and who is the loser. However, we all take losses and we all have opportunities to win. The work and time you put in and the knowledge you gain from the game will determine your victory. I have learned life is a marathon and not a sprint. There is a process for everything and we must take our time. One false move can change everything. The walk of shame is not a glamourous walk to take because no matter how much support, experience or money you have, you take that walk alone. No lie, that lonely walk has humbled the giant in me. Just when I thought I had it all figured out, there was another lesson for me to learn. I realized the learning process never ends and there is always more than what meets the eye.

They are calling my name now, the crowd is going crazy, and I feel love all around me. To see the smiles across the faces in this place is a great feeling, but they just do not know that this is the beginning of a new legacy. This is the family curse being broken and a new statistic being added to the book.

As I crossed the stage, the lyrics of my bro Obe Noir played in my head. He had graduated from college as well, so it was only right to applaud him. I guess we made it out okay to be from the inner-city blues. Even when they wrote us off, we persevered and wrote our own story. Many did not believe and some stopped believing, but we held on to our Faith. No matter how many times adversity showed up for an unexpected visit, we kept our heads up and weathered the storm. The OGs say that a real hustler can lose it all and find a way to get everything back and then some. It really pays being from the ghetto regardless of what society may think of me. I have two things no one will ever be able to take away from me: survival tactics and my degree. Clap for 'em, clap for 'em, Clap for 'em!

The road less traveled is a difficult yet satisfying journey. The numerous bumps, curves, roadblocks and hazards could cause anyone to stray away, turn around or go in the opposite direction. Not me. I am walking the walk that many only talk about. I often reflect on the times people used to laugh, point and make fun of me because I was and am different. I did not let that stop me; I instead persevered through the calamity. I do not think this narrative would have been the same had I not experienced life as I did. Who knows where I would be? I could have easily said to hell with the road less traveled and followed in line with the others. Then you all would have never received the opportunity to hear my beautiful rendition of the inner city blues.

CHAPTER 14
MY SIDE OF THE STORY

As I surfed my playlist one day, Marvin Gaye's "Inner City Blues (Make Me Wanna Holler)" began to play. If you sit still and really focus on the lyrics, you will hear the cries of my people from inner cities across the map. I can speak only on my ghetto, but I am pretty sure that many people can and will relate to my story. I can see Marvin's lyrics day to day in Southside Houston, TX.

From my perspective, I was born into a lacking and deprived environment. Though my parents worked hard and provided to the best of their abilities, I did not live in a fancy house in the suburbs. I could not afford to shop at the Galleria mall, so I had to stare at the shoes I wanted through a window, hoping I would be able to afford them one day. Even playing the dozens was all fun and games until you fell victim to the humiliation. Though you had to get in to fit in, those jokes influenced me to focus on the things I did not have instead of what I did have. It made me appear ungrateful to my family, but I truly did not mean any harm. Everyone else focused on what I lacked, so I naturally followed suit. Now that I am older, I realize I could have been looking at the situation from the wrong perspective—they could have been focusing on the shoes and clothes I did have. Perspective really changes everything.

We all know the universal grocery store rules our parents made us follow: "Do not look at nothing, do not ask for nothing, and do not touch nothing." Oh, I cannot forget the classic: "If you embarrass me in public, your butt is mine when we get home." As bad as they might sound, those rules gave me a form of discipline. I believe we have lost touch with instilling value and discipline in our children and we need to get back to the foundation of those principles.

Imagine how different things would be if we returned to principles from when my generation and my parent's generation were growing up. When we had to go outside to play but be inside when the street lights came on. When the next-door neighbor was able to discipline the child or tell the parents/guardians when they caught them misbehaving. It takes a village to rear a child and I believe our village died off when Mama Bea and the other old school grannies left this wicked place we call home. I do not care what anyone says, the hurt you experience from losing your granny is real and never gets better. I miss her dearly and hope she is proud of the man I am today. She made sure we were good when Mama and Daddy went to work. To this day, I am still recovering from the trauma of losing her. I am still recovering from the adverse childhood experiences I endured in my household. As I look back, I am honestly amazed I have survived the hell I have been through. I am glad I am a survivor because you all get to see my ghetto through my eyes.

Many movies, songs and news articles focus on the ghetto, but I wanted to give a true representation of the hood. Many do not and will never know what it is like to grow up in poverty with limited options due to unfortunate circumstances. Our education, wellness, resources and finances were all limited. In any given area where access to necessities were limited, chaos could erupt at any given moment. My household, along with many of my peers' households, was chaotic as well. During that chaos, you learn how to survive by any means.

I have witnessed people waking up bright and early to work one to three jobs in a twenty-four-hour span. I have witnessed people selling drugs and their bodies for income. I have also witnessed people stealing from and killing their brother just because he was in possession of something they wanted or absolutely needed. What about the children you may ask? Some thrived in these conditions. Some lacked the proper supervision, love and attention they needed. Some witnessed their families being assaulted or killed. Some had even assaulted and killed others themselves. Some had to grow up quickly and help raise their younger siblings. Some were forced into joining "the family business" to learn the ropes and to help provide. Too many children were misguided, miseducated and mistreated but still expected to do the right thing. No one should have to endure that amount of pressure at any age.

Who is to blame for this discrepancy? The ghetto blames the government while society blames the residents of the ghetto. It does not help us one bit when the media calls an area Midtown when reporting positive stories but 3rd Ward when reporting a crime. Such examples of gentrification influence the way the media distinguishes "us" from "them". How can you blame us for resorting to the very thing that we see on a day-to-day basis? How can you penalize us for being miseducated when we are deprived of the tools we need to learn?

Over the years, many schools have closed due to performance, but why were these schools not meeting performance during their operation? Maybe it resulted from the district providing old textbooks or from teachers not being equipped to teach students constantly in survival mode. I struggled to pay attention in class because I worried about the things happening at home. I also remember receiving an old textbook in high school to prepare for the AP Microeconomics test and was still forced to take the exam because the district had already paid for it. Weeks prior to the exam, the newspaper published projections of the passing rates for the AP exam with every urban school projected to fail, while the suburbia schools received high passing rate projections. Can you imagine hearing your family members and your school constantly telling you that you would never be anything? This was our reality in the ghetto. Sadly, many of my peers believed they could not do anything but sell drugs, rob people and go to jail. This was not living, yet this is how we lived.

One of my objectives is to shine a light on everyday living in the ghetto. Just as many people are conditioned to persevering and overcoming adversity, many others are conditioned to remaining stuck in their environment. As you take a walk or ride around every corner, you can see the same people doing the same thing and talking about the same thing. This routine becomes comfortable to them because it is probably the only thing that makes sense to them or offers them the security they have longed for their whole lives. I do not expect many people to understand this, but I just want my people to receive a fair chance. Though we are and should be held accountable for our actions, taking the time to understand why a person makes certain decisions can possibly help you understand why we behave the way we do in the ghetto.

I made it out and I hope I can be an example for many others like me. It is cool to be a scholar from the ghetto; it is cool to say no to drugs and to go to school. It is cool to be different and to do things you enjoy. Never let anyone tell you that you cannot and will not be anything in life. That is the biggest lie anyone could tell. Though we have different stories, the struggle is the struggle. No one struggle can top another's struggle as this is not a competition. If you want to compete, then push your brother to succeed, to be better, and to pass on this torch I have passed on to you. Remember, if you want to take this walk with me, then get up and walk, but watch out for the shit I once stepped in. Yes, you will learn your own lessons, but take heed to the lessons I have learned. Always be teachable because just when you think you know it all, there is a new lesson to be learned.

For the ones that do not know what it is like to live this ghetto life, take heed and ask questions. I promise there is a lot for you to learn as well. If you genuinely care, then stay down for the process. It is hard to trust a soul when someone has caused you lifelong pain. The conditions of the ghetto made us this way, but it did not happen overnight. It resulted from several nights of adversity. As a result, the judicial system should look beyond the surface of our actions instead of locking us up without rehabilitation. Mental health does not have a face, age or name. It affects us all.

If you feel a vibe from these blues, then keep these words in your repertoire and pass them along to whoever needs them. The ghetto has taught me that good dope sells itself. Education is my drug of choice and I aim to infiltrate every ghetto, household, street and demographic. This is my side of the story. Even if you disagree with it, I only ask of you to respect the ghetto.

ABOUT THE AUTHOR

Thaddeus Jamal Tolbert is the son of Michale Tolbert, Sr. and Gizelle Tolbert and the husband of Hophni Honore-Tolbert. He is a native of 3rd Ward Houston, TX and is extremely hands-on with the community. He graduated from Jack Yates High School in 2010 as the first of his siblings to graduate from high school. Thaddeus also graduated from Prairie View A&M University with a B.S. in Criminal Justice.

As a first-generation graduate, Thaddeus utilizes his experience to empower others, no matter their age, wage or stage, to educate themselves, to become all they have ever dreamed of becoming, and to help others join the race. He is currently a candidate for an M.A. in Counselor Education at Sam Houston State University and is pursuing many credentials such as the LPC. He is trauma-focused trained and has a passion for treating vast populations with various mental health diagnoses. Serving people is his passion and part of the reason #GHETTO The Inner City Blues exists.

Made in the USA
Columbia, SC
10 February 2023

11424397R00126